THE
LIT
BOOK OF
VERY
DIRTY
WORDS

Alexis Munier

adamsmedia
Avon, Massachusetts

Published by
Adams Media, a division of F+W Media, Inc.
57 Littlefield Street, Avon, MA 02322. U.S.A.
www.adamsmedia.com

ISBN 10: 1-60550-652-4
ISBN 13: 978-1-60550-652-4

Printed in the United States of America.

J I H G F E D C B A

Library of Congress Cataloging-in-Publication Data
is available from the publisher.

This publication is designed to provide accurate and authoritative information
with regard to the subject matter covered. It is sold with the understanding
that the publisher is not engaged in rendering legal, accounting, or other professional advice. If legal advice or other expert assistance is required, the ser-
vices of a competent professional person should be sought.
    —From a *Declaration of Principles* jointly adopted by a Committee of the
    American Bar Association and a Committee of Publishers and Associations

Many of the designations used by manufacturers and sellers to distinguish
their product are claimed as trademarks. Where those designations appear in
this book and Adams Media was aware of a trademark claim, the designations
have been printed with initial capital letters.

This book is available at quantity discounts for bulk purchases.
For information, please call 1-800-289-0963.

To Greg, Mikey, and Toby,
the filthiest f**king guys I know.

—ALEXIS MUNIER

Introduction

Ah English—if there is anything close to a perfect language for cursing, swearing and insulting, you've found it. English is not only spoken in one variant or another in the UK, Ireland, South Africa, Australia, United States, and the Caribbean, but it's also the mother tongue of more than a third of a billion *mofos* worldwide. Fortunately, English has borrowed from many languages over the years, making it the world's richest—and raunchiest—language, ripe with delectable dirty words. Unfortunately, unless you can really *shoot the shit*, you have some serious catching up to do.

You may think you're all that, but there's more to putting someone in their place than calling them *shitface*. Is he just not that into you when he calls you a *minger*? When that *biddy* says she's *chuffed*, should you unzip your fly or slam the door in her face? If your lover begs for a *chili dog*, do you stock up on beans or wet wipes?

No fear: *The Little Red Book of Very Dirty Words* is here to give you a deliciously filthy introduction into the netherworlds (and nether regions) of true American, British, Australian, and other sorts of forbidden English. Be it *cocksucking* in Cleveland or *leathered* in London, this hysterical collection of dirty slang, idioms, and colloquialisms will have you *begging for it*. So call *dibs* on that seat, get *plastered*, and channel your inner potty-mouth with the sidesplitting linguistic journey that is *The Little Red Book of Very Dirty Words*.

ACKNOWLEDGMENTS

A heartfelt thank you to contributors Matt Glazer, Jason Niemann, Gregory Bergman, Michael Paul Lee, T.S. Winn, Chris Robson, and Katherine Clinton Robson for their excellent work. Thanks as well to Mom, Emmanuel Tichelli, Georgina Bingham, Toby and Karen Ernberg, Yoann Unghy, Coralee Elder, Louis Da Drama, Bondy, Si, Jimmy, Alec, Big Gay, the Robsons, the Andersons, Derek Hambly, and David George, who all took the time to get down and dirty for this book.

—ALEXIS MUNIER

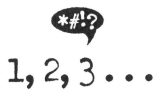

1, 2, 3 . . .

$1 + 1 = 3$, n.

the sex act as procreation; *American*

> The unconventional equation, $1 + 1 = 3$, reminds us that what takes two can produce a third—a baby.

3-way, n.

a sexual threesome, usually (but not always) two women and a man; *American*

> The images of a **3-way** with the tall twins from Texas haunted his dreams for weeks.

➡ Top Five Male Sex Fantasies
  1. Sex with two women at the same time
  2. Sex with two women at the same time
  3. Sex with two women at the same time
  4. Sex with a famous celebrity
  5. Oral sex (getting it, that is)

4-way, n.

sex that involves four people, usually (but not always) two men and two women; *American*

> Think of a **4-way** as a sort of Sexual Twister game in which you play for orgasms, rather than points.

69, n.

sex position in which partners give each other oral sex at the same time; *American*

> The sex position **69** is the ultimate tit for tat accommodation.

THE LOVELIEST NUMBER

Called The Crow in the Kama Sutra, 69 is a nestling of bodies that allows lovers to perform oral sex on one another simultaneously—a pretty picture that has been immortalized in countless images over the ages. One such notorious engraving allegedly created by the acclaimed Belgian painter Felician Rops in 1865 appeared in *Le Diable au Corps*—and was promptly banned *in France*. Imagine what they would have thought in Boston!

academic bulimia, n.

the act of studying or remembering facts really quickly without learning the meaning, so this knowledge can be regurgitated on a exam or test, but not retained after that exam or test; *American*

> I used **academic bulimia** to get by in college, so I could concentrate on the true meaning of college: sex, drugs, and awful mistakes.

aggro, n.

aggravation, trouble; *British*

> The missus gave me some **aggro** after I said her sister was looking sexy.

> My wife gave me some **trouble** after I said her sister was looking sexy.

agnosexual, n.

bisexual; *American*

> Somewhere between heterosexual and homosexual, the **agnosexual** is hitting on everyone.

a-hole, n.

slang term for asshole; *American*

> I called him an **a-hole** instead of an asshole, because my mother raised me to be polite.

aled up, adj.

drunk; *British*

> Robert was so **aled up**, he puked up in his mum's fake fire.

> Robert was so **drunk**, he threw up in his mom's fake fireplace.

alkie, n.

a wino; *British*

> She's such a closet **alkie**. She drinks wine for breakfast.

> She's such a closet **wino**. She has wine with her Cheerios.

anal sex, n.

copulation in which one partner thrusts his penis in his partner's anus; *American*

> **Anal sex** is not an effective form of birth control, no matter what your boyfriend may tell you.

angry dragon, n.

one who has been punched in the nose with a mouth full of sperm; *American*

> When klutzy Kevin came in her mouth, he smacked her in the face, and she shot sperm out her nose. One **angry dragon**, she kicked that man out of her bed.

arse, n.

ass; *British*

> Candice only let her boyfriend fuck her in the **arse** when he was nice to her parents.

> Candice only let her boyfriend fuck her in the **ass** when he was nice to her parents.

> **DERIVATION:** Arse comes from the Old English *aers,* meaning tail, derived from the Proto-Germanic root *arsoz* for anus.

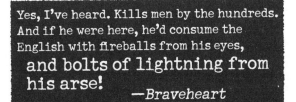

Yes, I've heard. Kills men by the hundreds. And if he were here, he'd consume the English with fireballs from his eyes, **and bolts of lightning from his arse!**
—*Braveheart*

arse-bandit, adj.

homosexual; *British*

> Sebastien is not an **arse-bandit**. He's just into arsefucking.

> Sebastien is not a **homosexual**. He's just into assfucking.

arseface, n.

ugly person, dogface; *British*

> Hey, **arseface**, move your bloody arse.

> Hey, **dogface**, move your fucking ass.

Asiaphile, n.

a person with a sexual predilection toward Asian women or men; *American*

> All of those middle-aged American tourists who haunt the streets of Singapore day and night are complete **Asiaphiles**.

ass, n.

beast of burden; buttocks; moron; *American*

> Tom wanted to fuck his girlfriend in the **ass** and she said, "You are aware my shit comes out of there," but he really, *really* didn't care about that.

> **DERIVATION:** Ass comes from the Old English *assa,* meaning donkey.

➥ Top Ten Most Beautiful Asses in Hollywood

1. Jennifer Lopez
2. Denzel Washington
3. Beyonce
4. Russell Crowe
5. Jessica Biel
6. Brad Pitt
7. Fergie
8. Usher
9. Cameron Diaz
10. Antonio Banderas

ass-to-ass, n.

the act of a large double-dildo being inserted into the asses of two girls, with the dildo penetrating the girls until they are "ass-to-ass"; *American*

> After that huge orgy last night, I woke up to find that the excitement hadn't stopped and two girls were going **ass-to-ass** in the living room.

ATM, n.

ass-to-mouth; the act of inserting one's penis in a sex partner's ass then sticking it in his or her mouth; *American*

> She told me she wanted to taste her own asshole so I gave her **ATM** right away.

attention whore, n.

someone, usually female, that craves attention at any and all costs; *American*

> His wife is such an **attention whore**—if she can't be the center of attention, she will ruin everyone's night.

auxter, n.

armpit; *Irish, Scottish*

> Hey mate, put on some deodorant. Your **auxters** smell like shite.

> Hey dude, put on some deodorant. Your **armpits** smell like shit.

B

baboon, n.

fool; *American*

I would never date his best friend because he's a **baboon**.

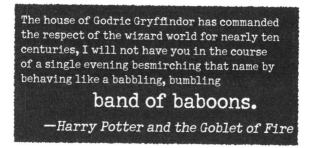

The house of Godric Gryffindor has commanded the respect of the wizard world for nearly ten centuries, I will not have you in the course of a single evening besmirching that name by behaving like a babbling, bumbling

band of baboons.

—*Harry Potter and the Goblet of Fire*

bad egg, n.

corrupt, untrustworthy person; *American*

Billy's brother is a **bad egg**—he probably would sell out his own mother if he could.

Bad bird, **bad egg.**
—German proverb

bagsie, v.

to call dibs; *British*

> As usual, Tom **bagsied** on that hot lady before I had even seen her.

> As usual, Tom **called dibbs** on that biddy before I had even seen her.

bahookie, n.

bottom; *British*

> Oi, I wouldn't mind that fit bird's **bahookie** in my face at this very moment.

> Hey, I wouldn't mind that girl's **ass** in my face at this very moment.

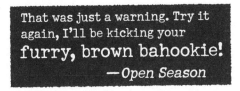

> That was just a warning. Try it again, I'll be kicking your **furry, brown bahookie!**
> —*Open Season*

balloon knot, n.

anus; *British*

> When she spread my bum cheeks and started licking my **balloon knot**, I almost shot my wad.

> When she spread my butt cheeks and started licking my **asshole**, I almost shot my wad.

banana split, n.

shit; *British*

> Let's wait before ordering a pudding; I right now have got to run to the toilet for a **banana split**.

> Let's wait before ordering dessert; I right now have got to run to the bathroom to take a **shit**.

bang, v.

to have sex with; *American*

> I just wanted to **bang** her, but she wanted a relationship. So after we fucked, I asked her to marry me. She turned me down flat.

> **DERIVATION:** The word bang comes from the Old Norse *banga,* meaning to hammer.

barmy, adj.

crazy; *British*

> Your old lady's a bit **barmy**, ain't she?

> Your girlfriend's a little **crazy**, isn't she?

barse, n.

perineum; area from balls to ass; *British*

> I got my **barse** pierced last weekend. It was a good thing I was fucking hammered at the time.

> I got my **perineum** pierced last weekend. It was a good thing I was fucking hammered at the time.

bash the bishop, v.

to jerk off; *British*

> John was **bashing the bishop** when his grandmother called, and continued jerking off after the call.

> John was **jerking off** when his grandmother called, and continued jerking off after the call.

bastard, n.

the literal meaning is a person who is born of parents who aren't married; derogatory term for someone you don't like; *American*

> Even if the **bastard** didn't sleep with my wife, he's still a **bastard** because, what, is my wife not good enough?

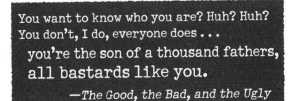

You want to know who you are? Huh? Huh? You don't, I do, everyone does . . .
you're the son of a thousand fathers, all bastards like you.
—*The Good, the Bad, and the Ugly*

bat for both sides, adj.

to be bisexual; *American*

> Winona **bats for both sides**, so Mitch really shouldn't even try hitting on her. He'd lose out to all that competition from both sexes.

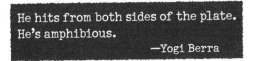

He hits from both sides of the plate. He's amphibious.
—Yogi Berra

bat for the other side, adj.

to be gay; *American*

> Don't get your hopes up, Alison, he **bats for the other side**.

batch, n.

single, bachelor; *British*

> I'm on the pull tonight. Is your fit cousin Eric a **batch**?

> I'm looking to score tonight. Is your hot cousin Eric a **bachelor**?

battered, adj.

destroyed; *British*

> Simon must've necked lots of E last night. He looks **battered**.

> Simon must've dropped lots of E last night. He looks **destroyed**.

bear paw, v.

to scratch oneself while reaching into pants; *American*

> The other day, Paul and I were in a restaurant, and he actually **bear pawed** his nuts in front of everyone.

bearded clam, n.

an unkempt, hairy, and generally unattractive vagina; *American*

> When Beth gets bikini ready for Rio, she trims her **bearded clam**.

beastly, adj.

nasty; *American*

> Jim woke up with a hangover and a **beastly** woman sleeping next to him. He vowed never to drink tequila again.

beat the meat, v.

to jerk off; *British*

> I like to **beat the meat** in the morning after a good night's sleep.

> I like to **masturbate** in the morning after a good night's sleep.

beaver, n.

pussy; *American*

> Her **beaver** was a forest in which I longed to lose myself.

Nice beaver!
—*The Naked Gun*

bee stings, n.

small breasts; *British*

> The French prefer **bee stings** to corking milkers.

> The French prefer **small breasts** to huge titties.

beef curtains, n.

a vagina whose outer labia is constantly swollen
and engorged from copious amounts of intercourse;
American

> On that first weekend together, we had so much sex
> that my girlfriend's **beef curtains** were big enough to
> hide behind by the time Monday rolled around.

bell end, n.

dick head; *British*

> My mate once shagged a girl who vengefully
> attempted to bite off his **bell end** because he said
> her new jeans made her look fat. He obviously knew
> nothing about women.

> My friend once fucked a girl who vengefully attempted
> to bite off his **dick** because he said her new jeans made
> her look fat. He obviously knew nothing about women.

bender, n.

queer, homo; *British*

> I have no problem with his being a **bender**, except
> when he tries to stick his goolies in my mouth.

> I have no problem with his being a **homo**, except
> when he tries to tea bag me.

bestiality, n.

sex with an animal or animals; *American*

> Hey, my dog isn't into **bestiality**, so don't get any ideas.

> Randal: You're in the bestiality business.
> Sexy Stud: Hey fucko! We like to call it
> **inter-species erotica.**
> —*Clerks II*

bevvied, adj.

drunk; *British*

> We were going to go for a couple more after the game, but I was so **bevvied** that I puked on a few of my friends and the night was over for me—and them.

> We were going to go for a couple more after the game, but I was so **drunk** that I puked on a few of my friends and the night was over for me—and them.

biddy, n.

a cute girl; *American*

> I want to tap that **biddy** with the smoking ass.

> **DERIVATION:** Biddy is a surprisingly flattering derivation of the derogatory word bitch.

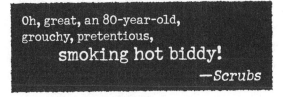

> Oh, great, an 80-year-old, grouchy, pretentious,
> **smoking hot biddy!**
> —*Scrubs*

biff, n.

vagina; *British*

> I think the bird who sits opposite me in maths is well up for it—she's always flashing me her **biff**.

> I think the chick who sits across from me in math class wants my dick badly—she's always flashing me her **pussy**.

the bill, n.

the man, the police; *British*

> I was pulled over by **the bill** last night for speeding and fuzzy dice.

> I got stopped by **the police** last night for speeding and fuzzy dice.

bimbo, n.

a stupid woman or man; *American*

> He got that **bimbo** to go home with him because he proved to her he was a doctor by showing her his toy stethoscope.

> ... I'm not gonna parade around in a swimsuit
> **like some airhead bimbo**
> that goes by the name Gracie Lou Freebush and all she wants is world peace ...
>
> —*Miss Congeniality*

bingo wings, n.

flabby upper arms; *British*

> Look at the **bingo wings** on Grandma!

> Look at the **flabby arms** on Grandma!

birdbrain, n.

stupid man or woman; *American*

> I bet even Steven could score with that **birdbrain** over there.

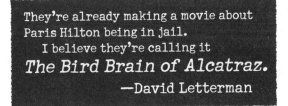

> They're already making a movie about Paris Hilton being in jail.
> I believe they're calling it
> *The Bird Brain of Alcatraz.*
> —David Letterman

a bit of crumpet, n.

a woman who is good enough to eat (sexual sense); *British*

> Tess is **a bit of crumpet**, and I would start with her arse.

> Tess is **the kind of girl I would eat out**, and I would start with her ass.

a bit on the side, n.

affair; *American*

> She knew he had **a bit on the side** when she came home early and found him screwing her Pilates instructor.

bitch, n.

a whiny woman or man; a person who is whipped into to doing whatever his or her partner tells him or her to do; *American*

> He's such a little **bitch** that when his girlfriend orders him to pick up her dog's shit, he actually does it.

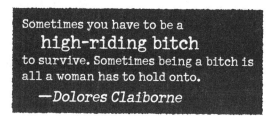

Sometimes you have to be a **high-riding bitch** to survive. Sometimes being a bitch is all a woman has to hold onto.

—*Dolores Claiborne*

the bizzies, n.

the police; *British*

> **The bizzies** have a lot of work to do in Liverpool 'cause half the city are thieves.

> **The police** have a lot of work to do in Liverpool 'cause half the city are thieves.

bladdered, adj.

drunk, wasted; *British*

> The groomsmen were completely **bladdered** on the wedding day after a wild night of debauchery that would make Hunter S. Thompson proud.

> The groomsmen were completely **wasted** on the wedding day after a wild night of debauchery that would make Hunter S. Thompson proud.

blast, n.

mouthful of smoke; *British*

> Stop bogarting that roach and give me a **blast** of it.

> Stop bogarting that roach and let me get a **toke**.

blaze, v.

to smoke marijuana; *British*

> Let's skive chemistry and **blaze** up behind the bike shed.

> Let's cut chemistry and **smoke** some weed behind the bike shed.

blinding, adj.

fantastic; *British*

> I went to see Radiohead last night. They were fucking **blinding**.

> I went to see Radiohead last night. They were fucking **fantastic**.

bloody, adj.

damn; *British*

> Get your **bloody** hands off me!

> Get your **damn** hands off me!

> **DERIVATION:** The word bloody is a very offensive term in England, where its derivation is still being debated. Some say it comes from a derogatory form of "blue-blood," used by commoners to put down aristocrats. Others insist that it refers to menstrual blood. Another theory is that the term is a sacrilegious variation of "God's Blood" or "By Our Lady."

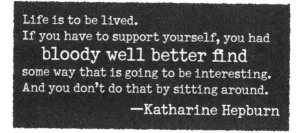

> Life is to be lived.
> If you have to support yourself, you had
> ## bloody well better find
> some way that is going to be interesting.
> And you don't do that by sitting around.
>
> —Katharine Hepburn

bloody vaginal belch, n.

a rarely seen phenomenon in which a woman on her period expels air from her vagina with enough force to be likened to a wet burp; *American*

> We were in bed, and she let loose a **bloody vaginal belch** that may have been the most hellacious sound ever heard.

blow a load, v.

to ejaculate; *American*

> When **I blew my load** on her face and didn't warn her, she kicked me in the balls.

blowjob, n.

a sexual act where a man receives oral sex; *American*

> She was so high last night that when she gave him a **blowjob** at the party, she volunteered to swallow.

blue balls, n.

soreness of the scrotum caused from a long period without an orgasm; *American*

> My wife has been holding out on sex for weeks; my **blue balls** may never go away.

blumpkin, n.

an act where a man receives a blowjob while taking a shit; *American*

> She was so shit-faced I got her to give me a **blumpkin**. Then she threw up in my lap.

boff, v.

to fart; *British*

> Brussels sprouts make me **boff**.

> Brussel sprouts make me **fart**.

> **DERIVATION:** Boff can also mean to have sex, so maybe Brussel sprouts put you in the mood for that too.

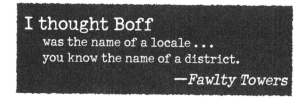

> **I thought Boff**
> was the name of a locale...
> you know the name of a district.
> —*Fawlty Towers*

bogging, adj.

disgusting, smelly; *Scottish*

> Get your **bogging** bollocks out of my face!

> Get your **smelly** balls out of my face!

boiler, n.

dog; *British*

> Ask Prudence out? Not a chance; she hit every branch of the ugly tree on the way down. She's a proper **boiler**.

> Ask Prudence out? Not a chance; she was hit with the ugly stick. She's a real **dog**.

bollocks, n.

bullshit; lit. testicles; *British*

> **Bollocks**! There's no way she'll let you have sex with her after you forgot to feed her cat while she was away.

> **Bullshit**! There's no way she'll let you have sex with her after you forgot to feed her cat while she was away.

> **DERIVATION:** The Anglo-Saxon word *bollocks* meaning testicles comes from the Teutonic word *ball*, meaning "to swell." By the seventeenth century, it was also used to describe priests delivering silly sermons—hence its current usage for "nonsense."

OBSCENITY CHARGES

In 1977, the Sex Pistols produced an album titled *Never Mind the Bollocks, Here's the Sex Pistols*. The punk rockers were later taken to court on obscenity charges—but thanks to acclaimed linguistics professor James Kingsley, the charges were dismissed. Kingsley convinced the court that the word bollocks could also refer to the clergy—and to silliness itself. And the Sex Pistols are nothing if not silly.

bollock someone, v.

to tell someone off; *British*

> My boyfriend bollocked me for staying out all night.

> My boyfriend told me off for staying out all night.

bone, v.

to fuck someone; *American*

> I want to **bone** that chick but I'm afraid my penis might fall off from all of her STDs.

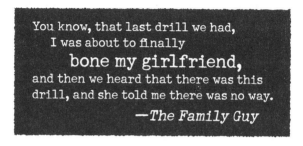

You know, that last drill we had, I was about to finally **bone my girlfriend,** and then we heard that there was this drill, and she told me there was no way.

—*The Family Guy*

boner, n.

hard-on; *American*

> His **boner** is tremendous, but I always get this awful feeling it's like fake tits because he uses Viagra.

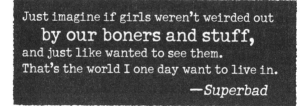

Just imagine if girls weren't weirded out **by our boners and stuff,** and just like wanted to see them. That's the world I one day want to live in.

—*Superbad*

boob tube, n.

tube top; *British*

> No offense, but your sister shouldn't wear a **boob tube** until she loses a stone.

> No offense, but your sister shouldn't wear a **tube top** until she loses fifteen pounds.

> **DERIVATION:** "Boob tube" also means television in America, so one could say, "If she didn't spend so much time in front of the boob tube, she would be able to fit into her boob tube."

booty call, n.

a call at night with the explicit intent of having sex; *American*

> Tiffany was always good for a **booty call**, but the logistics grew more difficult after she got married.

> That's what a girl wants to hear:
> 'Darling, do all the weird crap you like, just don't be late for
> **the booty call.'**
> —*Veronica Mars*

booze-whore, n.

a slut who uses a guy to pay for her drink(s) then leaves him with nothing but the bill; *American*

> That **booze-whore** tried to steal my drink right out of my hand, but I pulled the shot glass away just in time to gulp the whiskey down myself.

31

Brad, n.

shit, *British*

> Pull the car over mate; I've got to take a **Brad**.

> Pull the car over dude; I've got to take a **shit**.

brain nuts, n.

coined by former *Daily Show* correspondent Rob Riggle, this is the term for removing the cerebral cortex that controls fear and reason and replacing it with an extra set of testicles; masculinity; *American*

> Those dudes on *Jackass* have some serious **brain nuts** . . . also, they must be on *a lot* of drugs.

breasts, n.

mammary glands of a woman; *American*

> Nothing can bring a man to his knees faster than a beautiful pair of **breasts**.

SYNONYMS OF BREASTS:

appetizers	bazongas	boobsters
assets	bazookas	bosom
attention getters	bee stings	boulders
baby feeders	Berthas	bouncers
babaloos	biscuits	bottle rockets
bad boys	bombs	bra stuffers
ball sack rest rack	bongos	breasticles
balloons	boobies	brown eyes
bangers	boobs	bubbles

bull's-eyes

bumpers

bust

butter bags

cans

cantaloupes

Charleys

chest

chesticles

chitty chitty bang bangs

cleavage

coconuts

cupcakes

desk pillows

dirty pillows

dumplings

eye candy

flapdoodles

flotation devices

Fred and Ethel

fun bags

the girls

glands

globes

golden orbs

gonzos

grillwork

gunzagas

hand warmers

hangers

head rests

headlights

heffers

high beams

hills

hogans

honkers

hood ornaments

hooters

hot dog buns

hummers

humps

itty bitty titties

Jackie Chan and Bruce Lee

jiggly puffs

jobbers

jolly jigglers

jolly jugs o' joy

jugs

kaboobers

knobs

knockers

lactoids

the ladies

lemons

lungs

luscious fruits

mammaries

mammies

man pacifiers

mangos

meat puppets

melons

milk bags

milk duds

milk jugs

milk makers

milk wagons

milkers

milkshakes

moo moos

mosquito bites

mounds

mountains

muffins

nipple sporters

nodules

norks

nose warmers

the objects of my erection

pancakes

paper weights	sugar lumps	twin peaks
pears	sweater cows	the twins
pillows	sweater kittens	udders
puppies	sweater meat	water balloons
queen of the navigational beacons	sweater muppets	watermelons
	ta tas	wet tea bags
rack	teats	who let the dogs out
rib bumpers	tee tees	
rib cushion	Thelma and Louise	Wilsons
sandbags	tits	window washers
scoops	torpedoes	wobblesteaks
snuggle pups	Tweedledum and Tweedledee	ying-yangs
speed balls		
speed bumps	tweeters	Zeppelins

Bristols, n.

tits, *British*

> Do you see that fit bird's **Bristols**? Fantastic!

> Do you see that biddy's **tits**? Fantastic!

bromance, n.

platonic love between two men; *American*

> Sometimes Shelley thinks her boyfriend and his best friend Chuck have more than a **bromance** because they finish each other's sentences. As long as that's all they finish.

brown eye, n.

an anus, asshole; *American*

> George was an anal freak; as soon as she touched his **brown eye**, he cried like a baby.

bullshit, n.

nonsense or an obvious lie; *American*

> Most politicians have campaign promises that are **bullshit**, so don't expect that tax break to pay for all of your sex dolls.

> **Love is bullshit.**
> **Emotion is bullshit.**
> I am a rock. A jerk.
> I'm an uncaring asshole and proud of it.
> —Chuck Palahniuk

bum chum, n.

gay friend or lover; *British*

> Tell me that bloke in the pink sweater isn't your **bum chum**!

> Tell me that guy in the pink sweater isn't your **gay lover**!

bump uglies, v.

to have sex; *American*

> If I fail in my attempt to **bump uglies** with that pocket nymph over there, I'll probably instead just choke my chicken to Japanese porn.

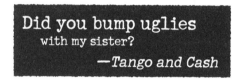

> ### Did you bump uglies
> with my sister?
> —*Tango and Cash*

bust a nut, v.

to ejaculate; *American*

> She's so hot that I would **bust a nut** if she just looked at me . . . uh oh . . . did she just make eye contact?

butch lesbian, n.

a lesbian who looks like a man; *American*

> I thought that babe was straight until I saw her lock lips with a **butch lesbian**.

butt

buttocks; *American*

> She had a **butt** you could serve tea on—and a Southern accent to match.

> **DERIVATION:** Old English gives us the word *buttuc,* meaning ridge—as in the end of a piece of land. Which is what your butt is—the end of your personal landscape, for better or worse.

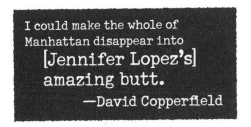

> I could make the whole of Manhattan disappear into [Jennifer Lopez's] amazing butt.
> —David Copperfield

butt pirate, n.

a man who takes pleasure in looting another man's booty; a gay guy; *American*

> Make sure he's not a **butt pirate** or you'll be wasting your time, Marge.

➥ Seymore Butts directed the acclaimed (in certain circles) 2005 film *Butt Pirates of the Caribbean.*

C

cack, n.

shit; *Irish*

> What a load of **cack**! Why would she ever want something put in that orifice?

> What a load of **shit**! Why would she ever want something put in that orifice?

camel toe, n.

when a girl's tight pants go into her vagina and reveal the camel-toe-like shape of her labia; *American*

> Wardrobe Rule #1: The tighter the jeans, the more pronounced the **camel toe**.

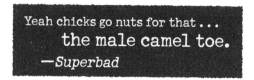

Yeah chicks go nuts for that . . .
the male camel toe.
—*Superbad*

candy apples, n.

a great ass; *American*

> I could bounce a quarter off that chick's **candy apples**.

casting couch, n.

any piece of furniture on which a man of power seduces a woman with promises of advancement; *American*

> The photographer brought the model back to his studio and, after he promised to make her famous, she slept with him on the **casting couch**. She should have made him take the pictures first.

caught short, v.

to have to go (pee); *British*

> I was **caught short** so I popped into the loo at the pub.

> I **had to pee** so I used the bathroom at the bar.

charty, adj.

disgusting, gross; *Scottish*

> I'd snog you, but your breath is absolutely **charty**.

> I'd kiss you, but your breath is absolutely **disgusting**.

chav

ghetto (white) trash; wigger; from the Romany word *chavi*; *British*

> The council house across the street is full of **chavs**.

> The projects across the street is filled with **ghetto trash**.

cheeky, adj.

smart-ass; *British*

> Wipe that **cheeky** grin off your face and make me a sandwich!

> Wipe that **smart-ass** look off your face and make me a sandwich!

cheesed off, v.

pissed off; *British*

> There's no reason to be **cheesed off** with me just because you caught me yanking my hard-on to your mom's picture.

> There's no reason to get **pissed off** at me just because you caught me masturbating to your mom's picture.

chili dog, n.

the act of a man defecating on a woman's breasts then tit fucking her, with his penis as the hot dog, the crap as the chili, and the breasts as the buns; *American*

> Pierre once lived next to a neighbor who was into **chili dog** and proud of it; Pierre subsequently moved as soon as he could.

chinless wonder, n.

snobby, rich man; *British*

> Look at that Porsche . . . no doubt driven by some **chinless wonder**.

> Look at that Porsche . . . no doubt driven by some **rich snob**.

choke the chicken, v.

to jerk off; *American*

> Bill was **choking the chicken** when his mother came home, so he hid in the pantry to finish up. It was a long night.

You choke the chicken before any big date, don't you?
—*There's Something About Mary*

circle jerk, n.

a group of men who stand in a circle and either jerk each other off or masturbate; *American*

> Stephan dropped by a friend's house with the understanding that there would be a **circle jerk** at his house, but when he got there, it was a baby shower instead. He should have kept his pants on.

the City, n.

Wall Street; *British*

> My uncle is a hotshot banker in **the City** by day and an aspiring porn star by night. Same difference.

> My uncle is a hotshot banker on **Wall Street** by day and an aspiring porn star by night. Same difference.

clever dick, n.

obnoxious know-it-all; *British*

> When you interrupt my story with what happens at the end, you're being a bloody **clever dick**.

> When you interrupt my story with what happens at the end, you're being a fucking **obnoxious know-it-all**.

 DICK The thirty-seventh president of the United States, Richard Millhouse Nixon, was such a clever dick that his nickname was Tricky Dick.

clit, n.

short for the clitoris; extremely sensitive area of a woman's vagina that can be sexually stimulated; *American*

> By the time, I found her **clit**, I was so drunk and exhausted I passed out right there.

DERIVATION: The clitoris goes by many names, but the clit word itself comes from the ancient Greek *kleitoris*, which translates as "the man with the key." This surprisingly playful and perceptive derivation suggests that Greek women are happier than most.

WHO DISCOVERED THE CLIT?

Impossible as it may seem, men have been arguing over who discovered the clitoris for hundreds of years. The Italian physician Matteo Renaldo Columbo claimed his discovery of the "seat of a woman's delight" in 1559; his rival anatomist Gabriele Fallopius (yes, that Fallopius) protested this assertion, insisting that it was indeed he who had discovered the clitoris. Some 100 years later, the Danish scientist Kaspar Bartolin debunked both men's claims, pointing out references to the clit that dated back to the second century. Of course, every woman knows that if anyone discovered the clit, it was Eve in the Garden of Eden.

All of my piercings, sixteen places on my body, all of them done with a needle. Five in each ear, one through the nipple on my left breast, one through my right nostril, one through my left eyebrow, one in my lip,

one in my clit . . .
and I wear a stud in my tongue.

—*Pulp Fiction*

---

clot, n.

moron; *British*

> The dickey-wearing Loren seemed sophisticated at first, but as soon as he opened his mouth, it was clear he was a **clot**.

> The dickey-wearing Loren seemed sophisticated at first, but as soon as he opened his mouth, it was clear he was a **moron**.

cluster fuck, n.

chaos created by a group of incompetents; *American*

> Every C-level management meeting is a **cluster fuck**.

> **DERIVATION:** Also known as Charlie Foxtrot, a cluster fuck is a military term used to describe disastrous situations caused by too many inept commanding officers. The cluster refers to the oak-leaf shaped insignia worn by the brass.

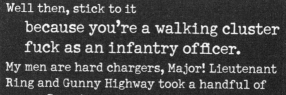

> Well then, stick to it
> because you're a walking cluster fuck as an infantry officer.
> My men are hard chargers, Major! Lieutenant Ring and Gunny Highway took a handful of young fire pissers, exercised some personal initiative, and kicked ass!
> —Heartbreak Ridge

cock block, v.

to block another person from having sex; *American*

> Just when the chick I had been trying to score with all night was sliding her hand down my pants, Al walked into the bedroom and **cock blocked** me.

cock tease, n.

a woman who continually leads men to believe she will sleep with them but doesn't; *American*

> She told me how much she wanted to screw, but the **cock tease** left after dinner—and before dessert.

cocksucker, n.

derogatory term for a man who is inferior to oneself; a person who gives blowjobs; *American*

> That **cocksucker** better get his SUV out of my spot before I key his car.

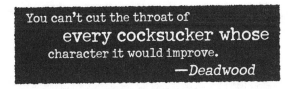

You can't cut the throat of **every cocksucker whose** character it would improve.
—*Deadwood*

codswallop, n.

baloney; *British*

> Stop talking **codswallop** and blow me for fuck's sake!
>
> Stop talking **baloney** and blow me for fuck's sake!

to come the raw prawn, v.

to act naïve; to bullshit; *Australian*

> Don't **come the raw prawn** with me, Enid; I know you borrowed my bike without asking.
>
> Don't **bullshit** me, Enid; I know you borrowed my bike without asking.

45

condom, n.

a contraceptive device made of latex worn on the penis; *American*

> If you're out of **condoms** on Ladies Night, you're fucked (or not).

> **DERIVATION:** Odds are the term *condom* comes from the Latin word for container: *condos*. But some insist that one enterprising seventeenth century Dr. Condom devised the sheath out of sheep gut to help His Royal Highness Charles II from spreading his, uh, seed throughout the land (Charles II had fathered at least fourteen illegitimate children at that time).

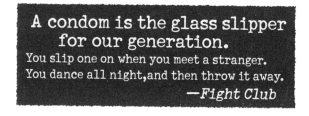

> **A condom is the glass slipper for our generation.**
> You slip one on when you meet a stranger.
> You dance all night, and then throw it away.
> —*Fight Club*

coochie, n.

vagina; *American*

> That biddy was practically shoving her **coochie** in Ben's face, but he was completely oblivious and ended up going home alone.

> COOCHIE
> The 2 Live Crew song "Pop That Coochie" is typical of the kind of music that came to be known as "booty rap" due to the graphic sexual nature of the lyrics. (Not to mention the title!)

cool your Joan Jetts, interj.

a phrase used by men to emasculate each other,
implying femininity; *American*

> So I told Michael, "Whoa there, missy, **cool your
> Joan Jetts**."

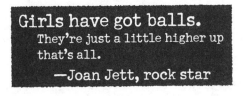

Girls have got balls.
They're just a little higher up
that's all.
—Joan Jett, rock star

cougar, n.

an older woman (sometimes a MILF), over 35, on the
prowl for sex with younger men; *American*

> This **cougar** was hitting on Rich outside of a club, but
> started talking about her kid, so he booked it out of
> there.

➡ Sexiest Celluloid Cougars
   1. Anne Bancroft as Mrs. Robinson in *The Graduate*
   2. Jennifer Coolidge as Stifler's Mom in *American Pie*
   3. Ruth Gordon as Maude in *Harold and Maude*
   4. Jane Seymour as Kitty Cat Cleary in *Wedding Crashers*
   5. Jennifer O'Neill as Dorothy in *Summer of '42*

cow, n.

a bitch; unattractive woman; *British*

> His sister is a real **cow**, but, you know, I'd still slam it.
>
> His sister is a real **bitch**, but, you know, I'd still hit it.

cracker, n.

derogatory term for a white person; *American*

> That **cracker** on the Lakers can't play basketball to save his life.

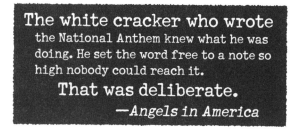

> **The white cracker who wrote** the National Anthem knew what he was doing. He set the word free to a note so high nobody could reach it.
> **That was deliberate.**
> —*Angels in America*

cracking, adj.

best; stunning; *British*

> I went home with a **cracking** girl last night and she ended up being a dirty slut.

> I went home with a **stunning** girl last night and she ended up being a dirty slut.

cream, v.

to ejaculate; *American*

> I **creamed** on her face after sex then went to sleep while she cleaned up. I never saw her again.

cream pie, n.

a vagina or asshole with sperm dripping from it; *American*

> We did it without a condom, and she had the messiest **cream pie** ever afterward.

crop dusting, v.

farting and walking simultaneously; *American*

> When I'm waiting in line and there are annoying people behind me, I end up **crop dusting** them with the hope that it will shut them up.

cubicle, n.

a stall; *British*

> The corner pub has a nice loo with three **cubicles** if you need to take a shit.

> The corner bar has a nice bathroom with three **stalls** if you need to take a shit.

> ➡ Take a shit in a cubicle in America—and you'll get your ass fired.

cum, v.

to climax; a variation of "come" considered a more obscene spelling; *American*

> Harold always yells "Jesus, Mary, and Joseph!" when having sex; he says it helps him cum.

cumshot, n.

ejaculation, usually on a woman's face, but can be on other body parts; *American*

> She still had some of my **cumshot** in her hair when we went out to dinner—it was a *There's Something About Mary* moment.

cunnilingus, n.

the sexual act of giving oral pleasure to a woman's clit; *American*

> Carole never performs fellatio on her man unless he performs **cunnilingus** on her first—it's a tit for twat thing.

> **DERIVATION:** This Latin mouthful of a word comes from the happy marriage of the word *cunnus* (meaning vulva) and *linguere* (meaning to lick).

cunt, n.

a derogatory term for a woman; *American*

> That **cunt** broke up with Ted by text message, and a second later she accidentally sent him a message meant for the guy who she had also been seeing.

SHOCKER

Considered by many to be one of the most offensive word in use in America, cunt was once described by feminist Germaine Greer as "one of the few remaining words in the English language with a genuine power to shock."

> You're not a bad person.
> You're a terrific person.
> You're my favorite person.
> But every once in a while,
> ### you can be a real cunt.
> —*Kill Bill: Volume 2*

D

damn, v., n.

to curse, to condemn; a curse; *American*

> When the priest says, "**damn** it all to hell," he really means it.

> **DERIVATION:** This word comes to us from the Latin *damnare*, meaning to inflict loss upon.

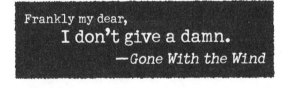

Frankly my dear,
I don't give a damn.
—*Gone With the Wind*

dangly bits, n.

private parts (male); *British*

> Trust me when my neighbour walks around his flat naked, you do not want to see his **dangly bits**.

> Trust me, when my neighbor walks around his apartment naked, you do not want to see his **dick**.

declare war, v.

to have rough, angry sex with someone; *American*

> I knew my girlfriend was cheating on me, so before I dumped her, I **declared war** on her until she had trouble walking.

debag someone, v.

to pants someone; *British*

> My first day in the dorms, a group of hooligans **debagged me**.

> My first day in the dorms, a group of bullies **pulled my pants down**.

deep throat, v.

in oral sex, when a man puts his entire penis down someone else's throat; *American*

> I saw a porn video where this girl **deep throats** an entire twelve-inch penis.

PORN CHIC

The 1972 movie *Deep Throat* was one of the first plot-driven porno films, giving rise to the term "porn chic." This groundbreaking X-rated flick asked the burning story question: How far does a girl have to go to untangle her tingle?

destroy, v.

to have angry, dominative sex; *American*

> He loved sex and also loved to be dominated; needless to say, I would **destroy** him on a nightly basis.

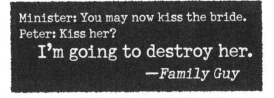

> Minister: You may now kiss the bride.
> Peter: Kiss her?
> **I'm going to destroy her.**
> —*Family Guy*

dibs, n.

the act of claiming someone or something so nobody else can take it; *American*

> Marcus called **dibs** on that chick at the bar, and none of us said a word because he was pointing at a billboard of the Miller girls.

dick, n.

penis; a jerk; *American*

> Dick is a **dick** with a nine-inch **dick**.

➡ Dick is a variation of the Old English moniker Richard, so commonplace a name that it came to mean "Everyman"—and every man has a penis.

dick around, v.

to do nothing of worth; to waste time; *American*

> Murray shouldn't **dick around** as much with video games, or his girlfriend will dump him and he'll have to create a cyber girlfriend.

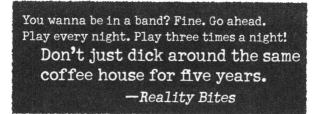

You wanna be in a band? Fine. Go ahead. Play every night. Play three times a night! **Don't just dick around the same coffee house for five years.**
—*Reality Bites*

dickwad, n.

jerk; *American*

> Not every Dick is a **dickwad**, but every **dickwad** is a dick.

Chill out, **dickwad**.
—*Terminator 2: Judgment Day*

Dirty Sanchez, n.

an act where a man wipes his penis on a woman's upper lip to create a mustache after anal sex; *American*

> I love a woman with a mustache, so I gave her a **Dirty Sanchez**. She was not amused.

documentary, n.

a discreet signal to a friend that there is a
sophisticated hot chick in ear range; sign to get a
sophisticated girl's attention; *American*

> Did you see that **documentary** about that girl, I don't
> remember her name, but she had handlebars and
> always wore a striped shirt.

dodgy, adj.

not to be trusted; sketchy; *British*

> That Alec is right **dodgy**. He's always hitting on
> underage girls.

> Alec is really **sketchy**. He's always hitting on jailbait.

dogging, v.

having sex in public; *British*

> The long-married couple kept their sex life fresh by
> **dogging** in Central Park on their vacation in New
> York City. But no one even noticed.

> The long-married couple kept their love life fresh
> by **having sex in public** in Central Park on their
> vacation in New York City. But no one even noticed.

doggy style, n.

sex from behind; *American*

> She had such a nice ass I just had to bend her over and give it to her **doggy style**.

MOO
The ancient sex manual known as the Kama Sutra describes several positions that feature what we think of as doggy-style fucking. The most famous of these is called the Congress of the Cow.

donkey punch, v.

to punch someone in the back of the head during orgasm when having sex doggy style; *American*

> The cocksucker tried to **donkey punch** me last night but I saw him move in the mirror and managed to duck.

doolally, adj.

crazy, eccentric; from *doolally tap*, meaning "camp fever"; *British*

> That sexy, short girl I brought back to my flat was fucking **doolally** in bed.

> That pocket nymph I brought back to my apartment was fucking **crazy** in bed.

WAITING
This expression comes from Deolali, India, where British forces were stationed during colonial times. Soldiers there suffered from a fever that induced delusions while waiting for their homebound ships.

doris, n.

girlfriend or wife; *British*

> We can actually hang out tonight because my **doris** and her friends are watching *Sex and the City* for the millionth time.

> We can actually go out and play pool tonight because my **girlfriend** and her friends are watching *Sex and the City* for the millionth time.

double clicking the mouse, v.

female masturbation; *American*

> When I came home and saw my girlfriend **double clicking the mouse** while staring at herself in a mirror, I thought, "I really want to have sex with that narcissist."

double fisting, n.

the act of fisting with both hands (putting both hands inside someone's vagina or anus); *American*

> He can't walk a straight line because he's obsessed with **double fisting**.

> **DERIVATION:** Double fisting can also refer to carrying a glass of beer in each hand at the same time. That's why your chances of double fisting your girlfriend double if she's been double fisting beer the whole night.

douche bag, n.

a person who is an asshole and not redeemable or
likeable in any capacity; *American*

> That **douche bag** not only cut in front of us at the bar,
> but also didn't tip the bartender.

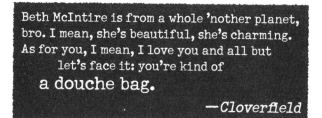

Beth McIntire is from a whole 'nother planet,
bro. I mean, she's beautiful, she's charming.
As for you, I mean, I love you and all but
let's face it: you're kind of
a douche bag.
—*Cloverfield*

douchepacker, n.

a lesbian who wears a strap-on dildo to have sex with
other women; *American*

> Maxine is into chicks, just not **douchepackers**.

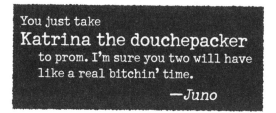

You just take
Katrina the douchepacker
to prom. I'm sure you two will have
like a real bitchin' time.
—*Juno*

DSL, n.

acronym for "dick sucking lips"; *American*

> That biddy over there has incredible **DSL** and I'm quite willing to accommodate her every wish for a blowjob.

duck butter, n.

sweat that accumulates in between a man's scrotum and anus; *American*

> Dude, it's so hot in here I could practically wring out my boxers from all this **duck butter**.

dude, n.

informal way to address another male in a positive way; *American*

> **Dude**, I call dibs on that chick, except if she's a lesbian—then she's all yours.

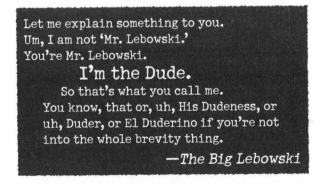

Let me explain something to you. Um, I am not 'Mr. Lebowski.' You're Mr. Lebowski.
I'm the Dude.
So that's what you call me.
You know, that or, uh, His Dudeness, or uh, Duder, or El Duderino if you're not into the whole brevity thing.

—*The Big Lebowski*

E

eat shit, v.

to humble yourself; *American*

> Whenever Darlene has had enough of her boss, she tells him to "**eat shit** and die." She's had five jobs in two years.

ego surf, v.

to surf the Internet looking for one's own name; *American*

> Andrew is so driven to be e-famous, that he spends half of the day posting and the other half **ego surfing** for his posts.

electile dysfunction, n.

the incapability to be aroused by any presidential candidates; *American*

> Ralph made it to the booth to cast his vote, but then he suffered spontaneous **electile dysfunction** and immediately had to leave without casting his wad.

emo, n.

a form of punk rock known for its mildly porno-
graphic, depressive, melodramatic lyrics; *American*

> You'll know **Emo** Eddie when you see him; he's got
> that curtain of black hair falling across his face and
> "Pretend You're Alive" by Lovedrug on his iPod
> blaring in his ears.

eye candy, n.

a very attractive person; *American*

> That biddy was pure **eye candy**, so hot she could melt
> everything in the frozen food section with just a look.

eye sex, n.

undressing each other with your eyes; *American*

> When Teresa and Eric looked at each other for the
> first time, that look lasted long enough to make him
> hard and her wet. **Eye sex** led inevitably to a one-
> night stand.

> Yeah, yeah, yeah, that's it.
> While you were cooking, you know, he was
> watching one of those, uh, those, uh, telenov-
> els, y'know, with all those ripe honeys on it?
> Y'know, he was really into it.
> I told you not to change the channel, man!
> Y'know, dude needs his eye candy.
> That's it!
>
> —*Breaking Bad*

F

face fuck, v.

when receiving oral sex, a man thrusting as though
having intercourse with his partner's mouth; *American*

> **Face fucking** is easier on those without a gag reflex.

fair dinkum, adj.

the real McCoy; genuine; *Australian*

> Wait, her lady-bazzers are **fair dinkum**? No bloody way!

> Wait, her tits are **genuine**? No fucking way!

fancy, v.

to desire; *British.*

> I **fancy** the pants off her.

> I'd **like** to get her in bed.

> Some desire is necessary to keep life in
> motion, and he whose real wants are supplied
> **must admit those of fancy.**
> —Samuel Johnson

fanny, n.

butt; *American*

> With a **fanny** like hers, the term fanny pack takes on a whole different dimension.

➡ Outside of the United States, fanny can also mean pussy, so think twice before you throw your fanny around overseas.

feel rougher than a badger's arse, interj.

to be hung over; *British*

> After the drunken escapades of my twenty-first birthday, I woke up **feeling rougher than a badger's arse** and puked up the eggs and bacon that my mum made for me.

> After the drunken escapades of my twenty-first birthday, I woke up **hung over** and puked up the eggs and bacon that my mom made for me.

fellatio, n.

polite term for a blowjob; *American*

> She was a high-class girl, so she actually used the term **fellatio** when she asked me if I'd like a blowjob.

> **DERIVATION:** Inevitably, this term comes from the Latin *fellare,* meaning to suck. Depending on who's sucking whose dick, you may be a:
>
> • **FELLATRIX:** woman performing fellatio on a man
>
> • **FELLATRICE:** woman performing fellatio on a man
>
> • **FELLATOR:** man performing fellatio on another man

filth, n.

police; pigs; *British*

> Watch out, the **filth** are somewhere nearby.

> Watch out, the **police** are somewhere nearby.

fingering, n.

the act of inserting your finger in a woman's vagina for her sexual pleasure; *American*

> The art of **fingering** is one every young man should master—and every young woman should enjoy.

HOLD IT In the Kama Sutra, a man who suffers from premature ejaculation is advised to caress his lover's clitoris with his fingers to the point of orgasm before penetration.

> If you need me, just call.
> You know how to dial, don't you?
> **You just put your finger in the hole**
> and make tiny little circles.
> —*Dead Men Don't Wear Plaid*

fit bird, n.

hot chick; *British*

> Let's get drunk, guys, and see who can kiss a **fit bird** in this pub. (Because fit birds just love drunk guys.)

> Let's get drunk, guys, and see who can kiss a **hot chick** in this bar. (Because hot chicks just love drunk guys.)

flash git, n.

showoff; *British*

> I don't know why Sue likes that **flash git**—he literally was wearing a bright yellow jumpsuit and dancing like he was at a disco.

> I don't know why Sue likes that **showoff**—he literally was wearing a bright yellow jumpsuit and dancing like he was at a disco.

flash the V, v.

to show the vagina; *American*

> This hot biddy named Tamora kept **flashing her V** to me while we were going over *Titus Andronicus* in my English class, which is just inappropriate on a whole other level. I'd still destroy that girl though.

> **DERIVATION:** In Britain, flash the V means to flip the bird, so a particularly vulgar girl could flash the V twice at the same time.

"V" CAN MEAN MANY DIFFERENT THINGS

The V sign in all its fingered variations (palm in, palm out, etc.) around the world can mean a number of wildly different things to different people:

- *Peace,* as in the "peace sign" popularized in the 1960s
- *Victory,* as used by Winston Churchill in World War II to encourage a besieged people
- *The letter "V,"* as employed in American Sign Language
- *The number 2,* when counting on your fingers
- *Air quotes,* a gesture with both hands that indicates putting a spoken word in quotes
- *Flipping the bird,* primarily in the United Kingdom
- *The Devil,* when placed behind an unsuspecting person's head as "devil's horns"

flippin', adj., adv.

term used to censor "fucking" in the song lyrics of
Flight of the Conchords; *British, New Zealand*

> I sometimes say to people that I am in fact the mother
> **flippin'** Rhymenocerous, but they don't get my
> reference to *Flight of the Conchords* and look at me like
> I'm a crazy person.

float an air biscuit, v.

to fart; *British*

> That bloody dog just **floated air biscuits**. He stinks!

> That damn dog just **farted**. He stinks!

frak (or frack), v.

term used on television show *Battlestar Galactica* to
censor the word "fuck"; *American*

> **Frak** you, if you don't watch *Battlestar Galactica* like
> it's your religion.

friar, n.

fuck; *British*

> Robin's a total bastard to his fiancée and he doesn't
> give a **friar**.

> Robin's a total douche bag to his fiancée and he
> doesn't give a **fuck**.

friends with benefits, n.

two friends who have sex, but aren't in a romantic
relationship nor have any of those emotions; *American*

> Maurice and Noreen became **friends with benefits**,
> until Noreen started crying every time after they had
> sex, and so now they're just friends with awkwardness.

fuck, v.

to have sex; *American*

> To **fuck** or to make love, that is the question upon
> which many a relationship may ultimately flounder.

> **DERIVATION:** The word fuck is nearly as old as, well,
> fucking itself. Some say it comes from the Greek word
> *phu,* which means to plant seeds. Under the Romans it
> became *fu,* as in *fututio.* That is, the repeated planting
> of seed after seed in a furrow. Some say that the word
> fuck most likely comes from the Old German *fuk,*
> meaning to strike, related to the Dutch *fokken,* meaning
> to thrust, and the Swedish *fock,* meaning penis.

> ➡ Fuck is arguably the most versatile and functional obscenity
> in the English language. The many fucking ways in which you
> fuckers can fuck with the word fuck are unfuckingbelievable.

ROMAN POETRY SLAM

The Roman word *futuo* was the poetic fuck of its day.
A favorite of the erotic poets, you'll find it throughout
the most licentious lyrics of the time:

> *sed domi maneas paresque nobis*
> *novem continuas* fututiones
> —Gaius Valerius Catullus (84-54 B.C.)

Translation: "But stay at home and prepare for us nine
acts of fucking, one after the other."

fuck, n.

jerk; *American*

> Look up "pompous **fuck**" in the dictionary, and you'll find a picture of a DMV clerk next to it.

Pulp Fiction. The Big Lebowski. Goodfellas. Boondock Saints. These classic movies (okay, well maybe not *Boondock Saints*) are all known for their colorful dialogue . . . but the grand prize winner goes to *Casino*, in which the F-word appears a record 422 times.

Fuck you,
you fucking fuck!
—*Blue Velvet*

fuck buddy, n.

a person who someone has sex with but has no emotional obligation like in a relationship; *American*

> For people who are congenitally incapable of long-term romantic relationships being **fuck buddies** is a fun and commitment-free alternative.

➡ Top Ten Fuck Buddies Wish List

1. Tina Fey
2. Jon Stewart
3. Drew Barrymore
4. Ryan Reynolds
5. Katherine Heigl
6. James Franco
7. Sandra Bullock
8. Will Ferrell
9. Amy Adams
10. Vince Vaughn

fuck like rabbits, interj.

to have frequent sex; *American*

> I'm surprised that either one of them has time to go to work because they **fuck like rabbits**.

fuck off, v.

to tell someone to get lost or scram; *American*

> I told that loser boyfriend of mine to **fuck off** forever.

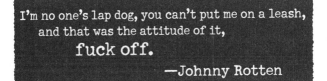

> I'm no one's lap dog, you can't put me on a leash, and that was the attitude of it,
> ### fuck off.
> —Johnny Rotten

fuck over, n.

to cheat or scam someone; *American*

> That judge really **fucked over** my ex in court. But I'm the one paying palimony.

fuck up, v.

to mess up, make a mistake; *American*

> We couldn't call our boss such a fuck-up if he didn't **fuck up** so often.

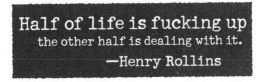

> ## Half of life is fucking up
> the other half is dealing with it.
> —Henry Rollins

fuck you, v.

common curse meaning "damn you"; *American*

> **Fuck you** and the horse you rode in on—that's what the cowboys say.

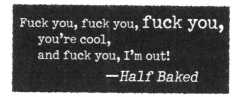

Fuck you, fuck you, fuck you,
you're cool,
and fuck you, I'm out!
—*Half Baked*

fuck-you money, n.

money that buys you enough freedom to do what you like; *American*

> The best kind of financial windfall is **fuck-you money**.

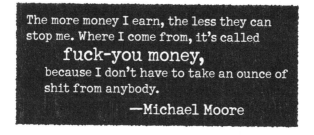

The more money I earn, the less they can stop me. Where I come from, it's called
fuck-you money,
because I don't have to take an ounce of shit from anybody.
—Michael Moore

fucking, adj.

used as an intensifier; *American*

> George Clooney is not just handsome, he's **fucking** gorgeous!

fucking A, interj.

short for "fucking awesome"; agreement; *American*

> **Fucking A**, that was a macking double overhead. Epic surf, dude!

fuckwit, n.

variation of nitwit; *British*

> If you're looking for a **fuckwit**, look no further than the House of Lords.

> If you're looking for a **fucking moron**, look no further than Congress.

fudge packer, n.

someone who likes to fuck someone in the ass (usually referring to a gay male but not always); *American*

> Doing it with a **fudge packer** can be really messy— not that there's anything wrong with that.

front bottom, n.

vagina, crotch; *British*

> When I was in my bikini, Jeff wouldn't stop complimenting me on my **front bottom**, the fucking pervert.

> When I was wearing my bikini, Jeff wouldn't stop complimenting me on my **crotch**, the fucking pervert.

full of shit, adj.

completely made-up, lying; *American*

> Craig was so **full of shit** when he talked about having sex with all of those supermodels.

gagging, v.

begging; *American*

> That dreamer Harold thinks every woman he meets is **gagging** for his dick.

> **DERIVATION:** Gagging can also refer to the (involuntary) reaction that takes place when deep-throating a dick.

gang bang, n.

a sexual act where a group of people (three or more) have sex with one other person; *American*

> Initially the head cheerleader was the main attraction of the gang bangers, but lucky for her the football team swung both ways—so when the so-called **gang bang** became an orgy of bisexual men, she escaped with her pompoms still intact.

get stuffed, v.

similar to fuck off, only not as harsh, meaning "no way!"; *British*

> You wanna watch *Strictly Come Dancing*? **Get stuffed**, I'm not watching that shite.

> You wanna watch *Dancing with the Stars*? **Fuck off**, I'm not watching that crap.

ghetto booty, n.

a big, firm butt; *American*

> If that girl's **ghetto booty** ran the world, there would be global peace.

Booty is just a ghetto expression, and I'm just a booty star.
—Richard Pryor

give a shit, v.

to care about; *American*

> I'm sorry, I think that you've mistaken me for someone who **gives a shit**.

Rehabilitated? It's just a bullshit word. So you go on and stamp your form, sonny, and stop wasting my time. Because to tell you the truth, I don't give a shit.
—*The Shawshank Redemption*

give head, v.

to perform oral sex on a partner; *American*

> So, she wouldn't **give** Marcus **head** unless he talked like William Shatner while she did it.

glory hole, n.

a hole in a men's bathroom stall in which a man sticks his penis through to be orally pleasured anonymously by someone on the other side; *American*

> What enquiring minds want to know: Was there a **glory hole** in that bathroom stall where Senator Larry Craig was allegedly caught making overtures to the undercover cop in the next stall?

go to town, v.

to have sex with someone; *American*

> If given the chance, I would absolutely **go to town** on that chick at the bar over there. And if pigs could fly, she'd let me.

gobshite, n.

a person who talks nonsense; *British*

> I'll need more lager if I've got to sit with my brother-in-law Matt because he talks such **gobshite**.

> I'll need more beer if I've got to sit with my brother-in-law Matt because he talks such **shit**.

golden shower, n.

a sexual act involving urination, generally a woman urinating on a man; *American*

> She told me her ex-boyfriend had a pee fetish and loved it when she gave him a **golden shower**.

➡ Golden showers feature prominently in a number of films, most notably Barbet Schroeder's *Maitresse*.

gooch, n.

a patch of skin between the balls and asshole; taint; *British*

> Shut up or I'll wipe my sweaty **gooch** on your face
>
> Shut up or I'll wipe my sweaty **taint** on your face.

goolies, n.

balls; *British*

> Tea baggin' is dippin' your **goolies** in an obliging lady's mouth.
>
> Tea bagging is dipping your **balls** in a horny lady's mouth.

gooseberry, n.

third wheel; *British*

> I believe I ruined Peter's chances of scoring with Diana because I was the **gooseberry** on their date.
>
> I believe I ruined Peter's chances of scoring with Diana because I was the **third wheel** on their date.

gormless, adj.

clueless; *British*

> That chick was all over him but he was completely **gormless** until I pointed out that her hand was in his pants.

> That chick was all over him but he was completely **clueless** until I pointed out that her hand was in his pants.

goddammit

to curse or condemn through heavenly intervention; *American*

> Watch out when the Colonel says, "**goddammit**." It means a five-mile march for all of us.

grizzle, v.

to gripe; *Scottish*

> My dad says Uncle John **grizzles** because my aunt won't stick a butt plug up her ass when they have sex—unless he will.

> My dad says Uncle John **complains** because my aunt won't stick a butt plug up her ass when they have sex—unless he will.

growler, n.

a hairy vagina; *American*

> I saw my roommate's girlfriend naked by accident once a decade ago, and I still dream about her groovy **growler**.

G-spot, n.

short term for the Graffenberg Spot located inside the front wall or anterior of the vagina and very sensitive to arousal; *American*

> Pedro failed so many times at finding her **G-spot** that he would just give up and play video games, so he could win at something.

➡ Top Five G-Spot Positions
1. Woman on Top
2. Doggy Style
3. Spooning
4. Reverse Cowgirl
5. The Peacock

> What's the difference between a golf ball
> ### and a G-spot?
> I'll spend twenty minutes looking for a golf ball!
> —In the Company of Men

G-string, n.

a narrow piece of cloth designed to cover the pubic area held on by a string; *American*

> Inside every woman, there's a **G-string** stripper dying to get up on a pole and dance every once in a while.

> **DERIVATION:** The original "geestring" was the 1800s-era term used to describe the string that held up the loincloth worn by Native Americans. By the 1930s, G-string also referred to the underwear primarily worn by strippers at the time. Pinup girl Betty Page caused a sensation in the 1950s when she donned her own handcrafted G-strings. Times have changed.

gully hole, n.

a vagina; *American*

> Chad's hitting on that brainiac, claiming that he likes smart women, but really he's only after her **gully hole**.

H

handlebars, n.

a pig-tail hairstyle; *American*

> Men go for that naughty schoolgirl thing, so Rhonda wears **handlebars** when she's trolling for profs.

hanky panky, n.

sex; *American*

> When you're serious about doing the **hanky panky**, you're not on the dance floor any more.

hard-on, n.

an erect penis; *American*

> Ronald took too many Viagra and ended up with the **hard-on** from hell.

> When a naked man is chasing a woman through an alley with a butcher's knife
> **and a hard-on,**
> I figure he isn't out collecting for the Red Cross!
> —*Dirty Harry*

79

have sexual intercourse, v.

to copulate; *American*

> Foreplay is fine for an appetizer, but **intercourse** is the hungry man's meal.

SYNONYMS OF INTERCOURSE:

attack the pink fortress

ball

bang

bash the beaver

be intimate with

beat

beat cakes

beat cheeks

boff

boing

boink

bone

break one off

breed

BUFU

bump nasties

bump uglies

bunce

bury the weasel

butt fuck

butter the muffin

chop up

clap

consummate

copulate

cornhole

creak the bed

dance with

declare war

destroy

dig out

do it

do the funky chicken

do the horizontal bop

do the hunka chunka

do the laundry

do the nasty

do the wild thing

dog

dukin'

explore the map of Tasmania

feed the kitty

fire

fluff

fornicate

freakin'

frequent

fubb

fuck

geit

get guts

get it on

get laid

get some booty

get some dippings

get some nooky

get some stanky

giggity giggity

give it up

go at it

go to bed with

grease

GTD

hang some curtains

have relations with

have sex

hide the German sausage

hide the salami

hit it

hit skins

hit that

hizzit the skizzins

hump

jazz

kertang

kick it

kill it

knock boots

knock it out

lay pipe

lie with

lock crotches

make babies

make happy happy

make love

make sexy time

make whoopee

piece of ass

pile

pipe

plow

poke

poonj

pound the duck

pull ass

put out

put the cat in the box

rail

ram

ride dick

ride the flagpole

ride the pink pony

ride the skin bus to tuna town

rock and roll

roll in the hay

root

run train

schtupp

score

screw

scromp

scuff

serve

shaboink

shag

shuck the oyster

skrog

skronk

slay

sleep with

spank

squeak

stang

stir up the yogurt

storm the cotton gin

swag

swap gravies

tap ass

twerk something

wax ass

whoo hoo

zig-zag

hen night, n.

bachelorette party; *British*

> For Tiffany's **hen night**, the girls hired a stripper who looked like Carrot Top, so it ended up being a very short party.

> For Tiffany's **bachelorette party**, the girls hired a stripper who looked like Carrot Top, so it ended up being a very short party.

hen-pecked, adj.

being ordered around by a woman; pussy-whipped; *British*

> Henry is so **hen-pecked**—he literally left his own bachelor party because his fiancée called and told him to leave.

> Henry is so **pussy-whipped**—he literally left his own bachelor party because his fiancée called and told him to leave.

> A husband is a man who when someone
> **tells him he is hen-pecked,**
> answers, yes, but I am pecked by a good hen.
> —Gill Karlsen

high maintenance, n.

a person who takes a lot of money and time to make happy; *American*

> That woman with all the Mr. T bling is way too **high maintenance** for my hippie buddy Sam.

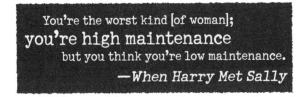

> You're the worst kind [of woman];
> ## you're high maintenance
> but you think you're low maintenance.
> —*When Harry Met Sally*

Hooray Henry, n.

brainless, rich, upper-class man; *British*

> Common thieves are more respectable than the **Hooray Henry** of the London Stock Exchange.

> Common thieves are more respectable than the **brainless greed mongers** of Wall Street.

hotbox, n.

a vehicle or closed room where the pot smoke doesn't escape and fills up the vehicle or room; *American*

> After a while of being in the **hotbox**, we had some serious munchies so we stopped off at a donut shop, and gracefully stepped out of the car, smoke following us, in front of some cops.

hotdog, n.

slang for penis; *American*

> When you're the **hotdog** for her roll, that's some kind of picnic.

Many of our evocative words for fruits and vegetables are sexual in origin (the very word fruit can refer to the child borne of a sexual coupling):

- Avocado comes from the Aztec word *ahuacatl,* meaning testicle.
- Vanilla comes from the Latin word *vaina,* meaning vagina.
- Tomato comes from the Nahautl word *tomatl,* meaning swelling fruit.
- Carrot comes from the Greek *karoton,* meaning horn.
- Fig comes from the Latin *fic,* which as slang could mean cunt, due to the resemblance to female anatomy when cut in half.

hung like a horse, adj.

to have a huge dick; *American*

> They may say size doesn't matter, but if you're **hung like a horse**, then you know better.

➡ The Four Horsemen of the Acockalypse
  1. Steve Martin
  2. David Letterman
  3. Billy Bob Thornton
  4. Eddie Murphy

I

Irish kisses, n.

the act of farting on someone's face; *American*

> Harry's girlfriend would often give him **Irish kisses** if he didn't wake up after the alarm clock went off.

Italian hanger, n.

a sexual position where the woman lies on her back and the man holds up her legs and feet during intercourse; *American*

> Ralph's flexible girlfriend finally talked him into doing yoga after she introduced him to the **Italian hanger**.

Italian Stallion, n.

an attractive Italian man who has a large penis; *American*

> Stella's boyfriend, Anthony, might seem like an **Italian Stallion**, but he doesn't actually know how to use his equipment for her satisfaction.

jailbait, n.

underage girls; *American*

> Hey, those biddies might want our junk but they are definitely **jailbait**.

jam sandwich, n.

police car; *British*

> Is that a **jam sandwich** behind us because only the bill could tailgate us that closely?

> Is that a **police car** behind us because only a cop could tailgate us that closely?

jizz, v.

to ejaculate; *American*

> Well, excuse me if it helps me **jizz** when a girl dresses up like a naughty schoolgirl.

John Thomas, n.

slang for penis; *American*

> When he told her his penis went by the name **John Thomas**, and could she please call it that, she laughed out loud.

➦ "John Thomas" was immortalized in *Lady Chatterley's Lover* by D.H. Lawrence. Originally banned for obscenity in Britain, the novel was published in Italy in 1928.

Johnson, n.

dick; *American*

> He whipped out his **Johnson** on the bus, but all he really had to do was pull on the chain to make the bus stop.

DERIVATION: "Johnson" owes its name to early twentieth century boxer Jack A. Johnson, the first African American to win the world heavyweight championship. When racist white America assumed he had a big penis because he was black, thereby accounting for his sexual prowess with white women, he allegedly stuffed his pants to good effect.

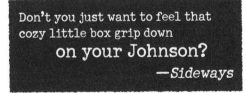

Don't you just want to feel that cozy little box grip down
on your Johnson?
—*Sideways*

juice the moose, v.

to fart; *American*

> Dude, you better roll down your window because I'm about to **juice the moose**.

junk, n.

penis; *American*

> My **junk** would fit into her DSL quite nicely.

junk in the trunk, n.

a girl with a nice large ass; *American*

> That dancing chick with the **junk in the trunk** at the club mesmerized every dude in the place with that sweet swinging ass.

K

killographic, adj.

containing violent content; *American*

> The wildly popular *Grand Theft Auto* is one of the
> most **killographic** video games ever to win the hearts
> and minds (and some would say souls) of fourteen-
> year-old boys.

> **DERIVATION:** The expression killographic was created
> as a label for "graphic depiction of brutal violence" by
> the National Institute of Media and the Family.

kinky, adj.

weird, in a sexual context; *American*

> **Kinky** is in the eye of the beholder.

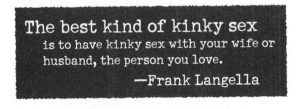

The best kind of kinky sex is to have kinky sex with your wife or husband, the person you love.

—Frank Langella

kickin', adj.

smelly, malodorous; *American*

> Since his girlfriend moved out, Sam went from well-groomed to **kickin'**—and his house wasn't much better.

knee trembler, n.

hurried sex while standing; *British*

> I had a **knee trembler** with her in the toilet, while her bloke was at the bar.

> We had a **standing quickie** in the bathroom stall, while her boyfriend was at the bar.

> ➡ In the Kama Sutra, lovers are advised to "feed the peacock" in a standing sex position designed for passion in a hurry.

knob-end, n.

dick head; *British*

> My **knob-end** is tender after last night's escapades.

> My **dick head** is sore after last night's action.

knocked up, v., adj.

To get a lady pregnant; being pregnant; *American*

> I should've wrapped it up 'cause now she's **knocked up**.

KY Jelly, n.

sex lubricant; *American*

> **KY Jelly** is the grease that makes the sex machine go round and round.

L

ladder, n.

run (in tights or pantyhose); *British*

> Oi, you look like a right slapper with that big **ladder** in your stockings.

> Whoa, you look like a real slut with that big **run** in your stockings.

lady-bazzers, n.

tits; *British*

> I would motor boat her **lady-bazzers** until I passed out from exhaustion.

> I would motor boat her **tits** until I passed out from exhaustion.

lairy bloke, n.

a man who ogles women; dirty old man; *British*

> The shuffleball court is always full of **lairy blokes**.

> The shuffleball court is always full of **dirty old men**.

lashed, adj.

drunk; *British*

> After failing my A-levels, I got **lashed** to forget my worries, or at least pass out.

> After flunking my exams, I got **drunk** to forget my worries, or at least pass out.

leathered, adj.

drunk; *British*

> You should've seen us at karaoke last night, we were absolutely **leathered**.

> You should've seen us at karaoke last night, we were absolutely **hammered**.

leg man, n.

a man who gets turned on by a woman's legs; *American*

> The longer the legs, the harder Sam's dick. He's a real **leg man**.

legless, adj.

really drunk; *British*

> I didn't think someone could get so **legless** on champagne, but Denise is truly a lush.

> I didn't think someone could get so **smashed** on champagne, but Denise is truly a lush.

lemon party, n.

three or more old, fat, gay men with flaccid penises in an orgy; *American*

> Everybody loves a **lemon party**—or not.

let one go, v.

to fart; *American*

> Whoever **let that one go** must've devoured week-old roadkill and washed it down with rotten milk.

Limey, n.

a Brit; *British*

> Sydney's full of **Limeys** these days. It's a disaster—from some Aussies' point of view.

> Sydney's full of **Brits** these days. It's a disaster—from some Aussies' point of view.

> **DERIVATION:** The term Limey comes from British sailors' use of lime juice to prevent scurvy.

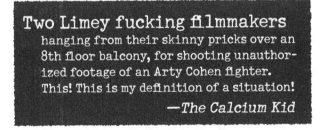

Two Limey fucking filmmakers hanging from their skinny pricks over an 8th floor balcony, for shooting unauthorized footage of an Arty Cohen fighter. This! This is my definition of a situation!
—*The Calcium Kid*

lingerie, n.

undergarments worn by a woman to arouse her partner; *American*

> I was aroused by my wife's **lingerie** but then wondered how much it cost; this thought decreased my arousal.

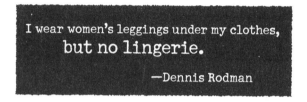

I wear women's leggings under my clothes, but no lingerie.

—Dennis Rodman

lipstick lesbian, n.

a lesbian who is feminine and attracted to other feminine lesbians; *American*

> When actress Anne Heche was going out with mega-celeb Ellen DeGeneres, the media dubbed her the most famous **lipstick lesbian** in the world.

liptease, n.

the act of putting on lipstick in a sexually suggestive way; *American*

> A well-performed **liptease** can prove as effective a strategy as its counterpart, the striptease.

London Bridge, n.

the act of two guys having sex with two girls from behind while the girls are facing each other on all fours and making out; *American*

> Many things have to go well for a **London Bridge** to become a reality . . . many more things for it to work. Thinking of the logistics involved gives a whole new meaning to **London Bridge** is falling down.

lose the plot, v.

to go crazy; *British*

> Mark **lost the plot** after he caught his brother shagging his wife.

> Mark **went crazy** after he caught his brother fucking his wife.

lush, n.

A person who gets drunk easily and, in most cases, flirtatious; *American*

> The difference between **lush** and lust is just one martini.

lust, n., v.

the attraction or desire to have someone; to desire to have sex with someone based on physical attraction; *American*

> I had a deep **lust** for the bartender, but when I found out she really enjoyed Battlestar Galactica, I fell in love with her.

to mack on someone, v.

to hit on, flirt with someone; *American*

> That hooker was **mackin'** on my husband so I popped her one.

mack-daddy, n.

a man who goes out with a lot of women; *American*

> Danny got three numbers at the party tonight—what a **mack-daddy**!

mad, adj.

crazy; awesome; *American*

> That was a **mad** party last night—I don't even know how I ended up waking up on the back porch with a dog licking my face.

madam's apple, n.

bulging Adam's apple on a woman; *American*

> Look at that lady with the mustache and the **madam's apple**. Gross!

Madame Palm and her five daughters, n.

masturbation; *British*

> It's **Madame Palm and her five daughters** for me again tonight because I ran out of money for whores. It's a tough economy.

> It's **masturbation** for me again tonight because I ran out of money for whores. It's a tough economy.

maki roll, n.

the piece of skin left over after a dog or cat is neutered; *American*

> Rex rolled over on his back in bed and, when I turned around, his **maki roll** was right in my face.

making an omelet, v.

A sexual act that involves ejaculating in a woman's ear, and folding it over; *American*

> I decided to be an asshole, so I came in her right ear and folded it over, thus, **making an omelet**. I am awesome.

mamma jamma, n.

something or someone very sexy; *American*

> Garth's new English Lit professor is such a bad **mamma jamma**—he's actually reading Chaucer in the original Middle English.

man boobs, n.

enlarged breasts on a man; *American*

> I'd do Patrick if he didn't have those awful fatty **man boobs**.

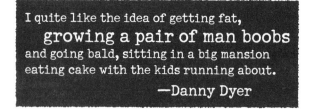

I quite like the idea of getting fat, **growing a pair of man boobs** and going bald, sitting in a big mansion eating cake with the kids running about.

—Danny Dyer

man cave, n.

a place where men can hang out without being bothered by girlfriends or wives; *American*

> Adam built himself an amazing **man cave** in the basement complete with a pool table, bar, and big-screen TV. He went down there three weeks ago and hasn't been seen since.

manny, n.

male nanny; *American*

These days all the cool celebrities want **mannies**, not nannies.

➡ Top Five Hollywood Mannies
1. Robin Williams in *Mrs. Doubtfire*
2. Tony Danza in *Who's the Boss*
3. Sebastian French in *Family Affair*
4. Hulk Hogan in *Mr. Nanny*
5. Scott Baio in *Charles in Charge*

manor, n.

neck of the woods; hood; *British*

Of course I know the way, arsehole—it's my **manor**.

Of course I know the way, asshole—it's my **hood**.

manscape, v.

to shave a man's body hair, esp. pubic hair; *American*

My girlfriend likes it when I shave my balls, so I **manscaped** last night.

manwich, n.

a threesome between two men and one woman; from "man" and "sandwich"; *American*

Yum, I'd love to be the meat in a Snoop Dogg and Flava Flav **manwich**.

Mary Jane, n.

marijuana; *American*

> Roll a spliff and let's smoke some **Mary Jane**, dude.

master of one's domain, n.

a person who can go without masturbating for long periods of time; *American*

> *Seinfeld* aside, I've never understood why one would aspire to be the **master of one's domain**.

masturbate, v.

to stimulate one's sex organs to the point of orgasm; *American*

> When you can't be with the one you love, **masturbate**.

> **DERIVATION:** While there is no certain derivation for masturbate, many believe that it comes from the Latin words *manus* meaning hand and *turbare* meaning to create chaos. Which seems about right.

SYNONYMS OF MASTURBATE:

Answer the bone-a-phone	Beating the bishop	Box the Jesuit (16th–17th century!)
Assault on a friendly weapon	Beating your meat	Buffing the banana
Backstroke roulette	Being your own best friend	Burping the worm
Baiting your hook	Blow your load	Butter your corn
Batting practice	Bludgeon the beefsteak	Calling down for more mayo
	Boppin' your bologna	Calling all cum

Carrying weight

Changing your oil

Charm the cobra

Choke the sheriff and wait for the posse to come

Choke your chicken

Clean the pipes

Clean your rifle

Clubbing Eddy

Couch hockey for one

Crank the shank

Crown the king

Custer's last stand

Date Miss Michigan

Date Mother Palm and her five daughters

Devil's handshake (Catholic school)

Diddle

Dishonorable discharge

Disseminating

Doddle whacking

Doodle your noodle

Do the dew

Drain the vein

Dropping a line

Dropping stomach pancakes

Fist your mister

Five against one

Five-finger knuckle shuffle

Flute solo

Freeing the Willies

Frigging the love muscle (British)

Getting in touch with your manhood

Getting in touch with yourself

Getting to know yourself personally in the "biblical sense"

Giving it a tug

Greasing your bone

Hack the hog

Hands-on training

Hand to gland combat

Having a Roy (Australian)

Have one off the wrist

Hitchhike under the big top

Holding all the cards

Holding your sausage hostage

Hone your bone

Hump your fist

Hump your hose

Humpin' air

Ironing some wrinkles

Jack hammer

Jack off

Jackin' the beanstalk

J Arthur Rank

Jelly roll

Jenny Macarthy jaunt

Jerk off

Jerkin' the gherkin

Jiggle the jewelry

Jimmying your Joey

Knuckle shuffle on your piss pump

Launching the hand shuttle

Making nut butter

Making yogurt

Mangle the midget

Manipulate the mango

Manual override

Masonic secret self-handshake

Massage your muscle

Massage your purple-headed warrior

Measuring for condoms

Meeting with Palmala Handerson

Milking the lizard

Milkywaying

Molding hot plastic

Nerk your throbber

Oil the glove

One-handed clapping

One-man show

One-man tug-o-war

Paddle the pickle

Pam Anderson polka

Pat the Robertson

Peel some chilis

Playing with Dick

Playing with Susi Palmer and her five friends

Play pocket pool

Play the organ

Play the pisser

Play the piss pipe

Play the skin flute

Play the stand-up organ

Playing with the snake

Playing your instrument

Plunk your twanger

Pocket pinball

Pocket pool

Polish the chrome dome

Polish the rocket

Polish the sword

Pounding your pud

Pudwhacking

Pud wrestling

Puddin'

Pull the root

Pulling the wire

Pulling your goalie

Pull your taffy

Pumping for pleasure

Pump the python

Punchin' the clown

Punchin' the munchkin

Punishing Percy

Punishing the bishop

Ride the great white knuckler

Rolling the fleshy blunt

Roman helmet rumba

Ropin' the longhorn

Roughing up the suspect

Rounding up the tadpoles

Scratching the itch

Seasonin' your meat

Sending out the troops

Shaking hands with Abe Lincoln

Shaking hands with the governor

Shaking hands with shorty

Shake the snake

Shifting gears

Shooting Sherman

Shucking Bubba

Slammin' the salami

Slappin' Pappy

Slapping the clown

Slap boxing the one-eyed champ

Slap my happy sacks

Slapping the cyclops

Slinging jelly

Sloppy Joe's last stand

Sloppy sign language

Stroke the stallion

Smacking your sister

Spank your monkey

Spear chucking

Spreading the mayo

Spunk the monk

Squeeze the cream from the flesh Twinkie

Squeeze the lemon

Squeezing the tube of toothpaste

Squeezing the burrito

Staff meeting

Stall clapping

Stroke off

Stroking it

Stroking your goat

Stroke your poker

Taking a shake break

Tame the wild hog

Tap the turkey

Tease the python

Tease the weasel

Tenderize the meat

The erky jerk

The sticky page Rumba

Threading a needle

Throw off a batch

Throwin' down

Thump the pump

Tickle the Elmo

Tickle the pickle

Toss off

Toss the boss

Toss the turkey

Tugging your tapioca tube

Tugging your tubesnake

Tug of war with cyclops

Tuning the antenna

Turning Japanese (UK— one step beyond wanking)

Tussle with your muscle

Unwrapping the pepperoni

Varnishing the cane

Wailing

Walk the dog

Walking Willie the one-eyed wonder worm

Wank (British)

Waxing the dolphin

Wax your Jackson

Whipping the one-eyed wonder weasel

Whipping the pony

Whipping the window washer

White-water wristing

Whizzin' jizzim

Wiggling your worm

Winding the Jack-in-the-box

Wonk your conker

Working a cramp out of your muscle

Working your Willy

Wrestling the eel

Wring out your rope

Wring your thing

Yahtzee

Yank my doodle (it's a dandy)

Yank off

Yank the yodel

Yank your crank

For the ladies:

Auditioning the finger puppets

Beating around the bush

Clam bake for one

Dialing the rotary phone

Engaging in safe sex

Get to know yourself

Get a stinky pinky

Hitchhiking south

Muffin buffin'

Paddling the pink canoe

Polishing the pearl

Tiptoe through the twolips

Washing your fingers

Reprinted with permission from *WTF? College*, Adams Media, 2009.

McJob, n.

a crappy job, often in the food service industry; *American*

> Now that the global recession's hit, I'll be lucky to find anything but a **McJob**, if that.

➡ One in ten Americans has worked at McDonald's, according to CBS News.

ménage à trois, n.

sexual activity involving three people; *American, British*

> My ultimate fantasy is a **ménage à trois** with Britney Spears and Lindsay Lohan.

> My ultimate fantasy is a threesome with Britney Spears and Lindsay Lohan.

WHEN IN FRANCE . . .

This term literally means "three-person household" in French, and implies that the three are one big couple. So unless you want to move in with your threesome partners, don't use it in France! To simply imply that you'd like to have sex with two other people at the same time, use the expression, *faire l'amour à trois,* to make love with three, instead. This way you're guaranteed a good time on a Saturday night, but spared the annoyance of not only one girlfriend or boyfriend, but two!

merkin, n.

pubic wig; *American*

> Kate Winslet has been quoted as saying that she was
> asked to wear a **merkin** during the sex scenes in *The
> Reader,* but declined. No wonder she won an Oscar for
> that role.

> **DERIVATION:** The word merkin probably comes from
> the obsolete English word *malkin*, meaning mop.

> ➥ Women started wearing merkins back in the 1400s—some
> because they'd shaved their pubic hair to prevent pubic lice, and
> others to hide the symptoms of venereal disease.

metrosexual, n., adj.

a well-groomed urban man who dresses stylishly and
draws comparisons to homosexuals; *American*

> My boss isn't gay; he just likes his accessories to
> match his outfit—a typical **metrosexual**.

microrgasm, n.

a small, quiet, short orgasm that lacks satisfaction;
American

> If Juan got a **microrgasm** out of his high maintenance
> girlfriend, he felt like it was at least a small triumph;
> of course, he did tell his friends that he had her
> screaming all night long.

miffed, adj.

fed up; *American*

> Christine was so **miffed** with her husband's bad behavior that she refused sex for a week.

MILF, n.

acronym for "Mother I'd Like (to) Fuck"; *American*

> Check out the juicy ass on Tanya's mom. She's a **MILF**.

milkshake, n.

body; *American*

> Tyra's **milkshake** is damn sexy—look at that big booty!

> **DERIVATION:** The term milkshake in this context was made popular in the Kelis song of the same name. The simplistic song features few lyrics, all of which focus on whose milkshake is the best. Despite this fact, the single was a hit worldwide, reaching number three in the U.S. and number two in the United Kingdom, in addition to being in the top ten in the Netherlands, Belgium, Sweden, and New Zealand.

mimbo, n.

male bimbo; *American*

> That hot surfer is a real **mimbo**: Body by Nautilus, brains by Mattel.

> **DERIVATION:** This term was popularized in "The Stall" episode of *Seinfeld*.

minder, n.

a bodyguard; a security guard; *British*

> You should've seen the size of Beckham's **minder**—he could have kicked my ass worse than his employer.

> You should've seen the size of Beckham's **bodyguard**—he could have kicked my ass worse than his employer.

Moaning Minnie, n.

a whiner; *British*

> Don't be such a **Moaning Minnie** and wingman for me so I get that fit bird.

> Don't be such a **whiner** and wingman for me so I get that sexy biddy.

mollycoddled, v.

babied; *British*

> No wonder Will is immature—his mother has **mollycoddled** him all his life.

> No wonder Will is immature—his mother has **babied** him all his life.

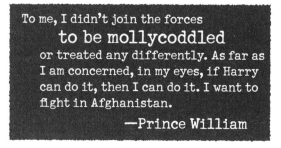

To me, I didn't join the forces **to be mollycoddled** or treated any differently. As far as I am concerned, in my eyes, if Harry can do it, then I can do it. I want to fight in Afghanistan.

—Prince William

moobs, n.

man boobs; *American*

> Victor thought chicks were jealous of his massive **moobs**, and never second-guessed himself.

moose, n.

dog; *British*

> Clara may be a **moose**, but she does have nice baps.

> Clara may be a **dog**, but she does have nice tits.

motherfucker, n.

a terrible or contemptible person; a jerk; *American*

> Tell that **motherfucker** to bring back my bike that he stole or I'll call the police!

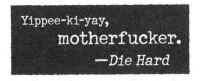

Yippee-ki-yay, **motherfucker.**
—*Die Hard*

muff, n.

female pubic area; *American*

> Isn't that cute, she's shaved her **muff** into a heart for Valentine's Day.

> **DERIVATION:** The word muff comes from the Old French *moufle,* meaning mitten.

muff diving, n.

cunnilingus; *American*

> The latest entry on newly married Brian's "Honey, Do" list: **muff diving**.

muffin top, n.

fat roll hanging over the waistband of a person's too-tight jeans; *American*

> If only Tania would buy her jeans another size up, she could avoid that nasty **muffin top**.

mug, n.

a person who is easy to fool; *British*

> Strangely, even though she's wearing that stupid hat with the feathers, she's not a **mug**.

> Strangely, even though she's wearing that stupid hat with the feathers, she's not a **fool**.

mutt's nuts, adj.

fantastic; *British*

> Sally's eyes are still the **mutt's nuts**, even when she wears too much eyeliner.

> Sally's eyes are still **fantastic**, even when she wears too much eyeliner.

N

naff, adj.

lame, crap; in poor taste; *British*

> A girl who gets uppity and rude about a guy opening the door for her is **naff**, so you should let it slam her in her face.

> A girl who gets uppity and rude about a guy opening the door for her is **lame**, so you should let it slam her in her face.

to narc, v.

to inform on someone; *American*

> When he got so stoned he missed school, Roger's little brother **narced** Roger out to his parents and he got grounded for a month. He'll never give his little brother any weed again.

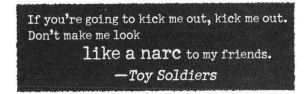

If you're going to kick me out, kick me out. Don't make me look **like a narc** to my friends.
—*Toy Soldiers*

nancy (or nancy boy), n.

pathetic person; homosexual; *British*

> Don't be such a **nancy** and get in the ocean—you've got a wetsuit on!

> Don't be such a **pathetic person** and get in the ocean—you've got a wetsuit on!

narked, adj.

pissed off; *British*

> When Ewan got dumped for merely looking at another chick's ass, he was really **narked**.

> When Ewan got dumped for merely looking at another chick's ass, he was really **pissed off**.

nasty, adj.

cool; *American*

> *Grand Theft Auto* is the **nastiest** game; my little brother plays it night and day.

necrophilia, n.

the act of having sexual intercourse with a human corpse; *American*

> If someone has sex with a zombie, technically that person is into **necrophilia**, and has way too many issues to solve in a lifetime of therapy.

to nick, v.

to steal; *British*

> You really shouldn't **nick** that dog—nobody on this planet would pay money for that unruly creature.

> You really shouldn't **steal** that dog—nobody on this planet would pay money for that unruly creature.

nimrod, n.

moron; *American*

> I couldn't believe Sarah married that **nimrod**, even if he was hung like a horse.

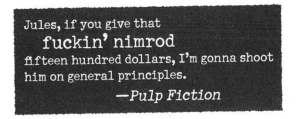

> Jules, if you give that **fuckin' nimrod** fifteen hundred dollars, I'm gonna shoot him on general principles.
> —*Pulp Fiction*

nonce, n.

pedophile; *British*

> Did you see the old geezer in that banger? He's definitely a **nonce** and nobody should ever accept candy from him.

> Did you see the old guy in that car? He's definitely a **pedophile** and nobody should ever accept candy from him.

not batting with a full wicket, v., adj.

not playing with a full deck; crazy; *British*

> Rob should never be your wingman because he's **not playing with a full wicket**, and might say something really insulting to your romantic interest.

> Rob should never be your wingman because he's **not playing with a full deck**, and might say something really insulting to your romantic interest.

to not give a toss, v.

to not give a shit; *British*

> Sorry, but I **don't give a toss** what you got for your birthday.

> Sorry, but I **don't give a shit** what you got for your birthday.

not the sharpest tool in the box, adj.

unintelligent, stupid; *British*

> I met my new boss today, and let's just say he's **not the sharpest tool in the box**.

> I met my new boss today, and let's just say he's **stupid**.

nunya, adv.

none of your business; *American*

> My wife kept asking too many questions, so I said, "You know what? **Nunya!**"

nut hangers, n.

really tight pants, mostly jeans, worn by guys;
American

> I really hope that hipster with the **nut hangers** loses
> circulation and falls over so he can serve as a warning
> to all of those other kids.

to nut someone, v.

to head butt someone; *British*

> Do that again and I'll **nut** ya like I'm Zinedine Zidane
> in a football match.

> Do that again and I'll **head butt** ya like I'm Zinedine
> Zidane in a soccer game.

nutsack, n.

scrotum; *American*

> If you want her to suck your balls, you'd better shave
> your **nutsack**.

nuts, n.

testicles; *American*

> It makes his wife nuts when he scratches his **nuts** in
> public.

nutter, n.

mentally deranged person; *British*

> That half-naked dude who was walking down the middle of the street and talking to himself was a real **nutter**.

> That half-naked dude who was walking down the middle of the street and rapping to himself was a real **loony**.

nympho, n.

a woman obsessed with sex; short for nymphomaniac; *American*

> I told that **nympho** to get her hands off my ass but she wouldn't listen.

A FUROR UNLEASHED

In 1775 the French physician M.D.T. Bienville wrote a paper titled "Nymphomania, or a Dissertation Concerning the Furor Uterinus." In this seminal work, he combined the Greek word for bride (*nymphe*) with the Greek word for madness (*mania*) to describe a "female disease characterized by morbid and uncontrollable sexual desire."

> **A nymphomaniac**
> is a woman as obsessed with sex
> as the average man.
> —Mignon McLaughlin

O face, n.

the face made when having an orgasm; *American*

Have you ever seen an old Ron Jeremy porno? What a homely **O face**!

> I'm thinking I might take that new chick from Logistics. If things go well I might be **showing her my O-face.**
> 'Oh . . . Oh . . . Oh!'
> You know what I'm talkin' about. 'Oh!'
> —*Office Space*

off one's trolley, adj.

fucked up; out of one's mind; *British*

You should've seen me at the bar last night—I was **off my fucking trolley**.

You should've seen me at the bar last night—I was **fucked up**.

off the twig, adj.

dead; *British*

> Somebody come quick! My budgerigar is **off the twig**!

> Somebody come quick! My parakeet is **dead**!

> **DERIVATION:** This is a reference to the famous *Monty Python* "dead parrot" skit.

offer someone out, v.

challenge someone to fight; *British*

> I'd had enough of him telling me how much he wanted my sister, so I **offered him out**. I don't actually have a sister, but it's the principle of the matter.

> I'd had enough of him telling me how much he wanted my sister, so I **challenged him to a fight**. I don't actually have a sister, but it's the principle of the matter.

oi, interj.

meaning "hey"; *British*

> **Oi**, you shouldn't knock fucking someone in a graveyard until you've tried it!

> **Hey**, you shouldn't knock fucking someone in a graveyard until you've tried it!

old chap, n.

penis; *British*

> My **old chap**'s covered in warts, which isn't a good sign.

> My **penis**'s covered in warts, which isn't a good sign.

the old slap and tickle, n.

sex; *British*

> No, your friend can't have **the old slap and tickle** with my mother while you watch.

> No, your friend can't have **sex** with my mother while you watch.

on the rag, adj.

menstruating; *American*

> I was about to go down on her, but she told me she was **on the rag**, so I fell asleep defeated.

one-eyed snake, n.

penis; *American*

> Why don't you come on over here and pet my **one-eyed snake**?

I used to call it stroking the salami,
yeah, you know, pounding the old pud.
I never did it with baked goods,
but you know your uncle Mort,
he pets the one-eyed snake
five to six times a day.

—*American Pie*

---

one-night stand, n.

the act of sleeping with someone for a night with no intentions of anything beyond that one night; *American*

> After our **one-night stand**, I asked her if she wanted coffee. She said, "No! Stop smothering me!" I was glad this would be the only time that I ever slept with her.

orchard, n.

two or more sisters with nice asses; *American*

> When those sisters with the **orchard** walk down the street, heads turn.

orgasm, n.

climax; *American*

> The **orgasm** is not the end all and be all of sex, it just feels that way.

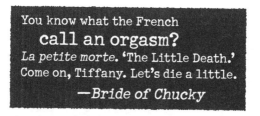

You know what the French
call an orgasm?
La petite morte. 'The Little Death.'
Come on, Tiffany. Let's die a little.
—*Bride of Chucky*

out of one's tree, adj.

crazy; *British*

> He did too many mushrooms, mate, and was **out of his tree**.

> He did too many mushrooms, dude, and was **crazy**.

P

packie, v.

a liquor store (used primarily in New England);
American

> Jason ran out of whiskey on a Sunday night and had a
> panic attack because when he drove to the **packie**, it
> was closed.

packing a gun and a holster, adj.

to be a hermaphrodite; *American*

> When I learned she had been born **packing a gun
> and a holster**, I really hoped she rid herself of the
> penis and kept the vagina.

> When she was born, she was packing both
> ## a gun and a holster.
> —*Freaks and Geeks*

parentnoia, n.

paranoia that a parent feels with regards to their children; *American*

> Cindy's mom had such a bad case of **parentnoia** that she read her diary to find out whether her daughter was still a virgin or not.

pecker, n.

penis; *American*

> Hannah was so impressed with her science class partner's **pecker**, she told all of her friends about it.

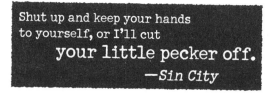

Shut up and keep your hands to yourself, or I'll cut **your little pecker off.**
—Sin City

penis, n.

male reproductive organ; *American*

> Mary was shocked at the size of John's **penis**; she didn't realize they came that small.

SYNONYMS OF PENIS:

5.9	beef bayonet	boa
34-25	beef hammer	boner
baby arm	bell on a pole	bossman
baby-maker	big enchilada	bratwurst
baloney pony	bishop	bud

burrito

cack

Captain Winkie

chang a lang

chank

chep

choad

chopper

chub

chut

cock

coque

custard launcher

the D

D train

dagger

dick

dickie

dicky mo

Diesl

ding dong

ding-a-ling

dingis

doder

dog head

doinker

dokey

dome piece

dong

donkey rope

dork

doty

dragon

dugan

egg roll

family jewels

fang

ferret

fire hose

fish stick

flesh arrow

foo-foo

frankfurter

fuck rod

fuck stick

gadoon

German sausage

god warrior

goot

hang dang

hard hat

Harry Johnson

Harry Wang

heat-seeking love missile

heli

hocky cocky

hoftie

hog

horn

hose

hot dog

injector

inserter

Italian sausage

jack hammer

jack in the box

jimber

Jimmy

jizz rod

jizz whistle

John Thomas

Johnson

journey stick

joystick

juice cord

junk

kickstand

knob

kontol

Krull the Warrior King

kur

Larry

leaky hose

lingham

little Elvis

the little head

little soldier

lizard

Logan

long john

longfellow

love muscle

love shaft

love stick

magic wand

male member

male organ

man cheddar

man crank

man horn

man meat

meat popsicle

meat stick

meat train

member

microphone

middle stump

missile launcher

Mr. Happy

monkey

murton

mushroom head

mutton

my Army stick

my little pony

my other half

my other head

my twig
(and berries)

NOFL

noodle

old boy

old fellow

old man

one-eyed
monster

one-eyed
trouser snake

one-eyed
yogurt chucker

p-nas

package

packer

pecker

peen

peeper

pene

penicorn

Percy

peter

phallus member

piece

pik

pingy-lingy

pink link

pinto

pipesicle

Pippen the Great

Pippen the Small

piss weasel

piston

plonker

pole

power drill

prick

private eye

pudd

purple people
pleaser

purple-headed
soldier man

purple-headed
warrior

purple-helmeted warrior of love

pussy factory

putz

Richard

rod

rod of pleasure

rubbing machine

salamander

salami

schlittle

schlong

schlort

schmeckel

schmuck

schu-bunny

sconge

scrotum

shaft

short arm

skin chimney

skin flute

snake

soup bone

spam popsicle

sperm pump

spike

Staff Captain

steamin' semen roadway

stick

stiffy

summer sausage

sword

Tallyrand

tallywacker

tassle

thing

third leg

thumper

tinky

todger

tonk

tool

tube steak

Twinkie

wand of light

wang

wankie

wedding tackle

weenie

wee-wee

weiner

whang

who who dilly

wii

willy

Wilson

wing dang doodle

wingwong

winky

ying-yang

yogurt gun

you're welcome

percy, n.

penis; *British*

> Adam's **percy** is a bit on the small side if you ask me.

> Adam's **penis** is a bit on the small side if you ask me.

personalities, n.

breasts; *British*

> Adrienne's **personalities** are her best asset.

> Adrienne's **boobs** are her best asset.

piece of piss, adj.

easy as pie; *British*

> That final math exam was a **piece of piss**, especially because I wasn't hung over for the first time this semester.

> That final math test was **easy as pie**, especially because I wasn't hung over for the first time this semester.

> It must be a lot easier being gay. Sex must be **a piece of piss if you're gay.**
> —*Coupling*

pig, n.

policeman; *American*

> Why is it again that **pigs** love donuts?

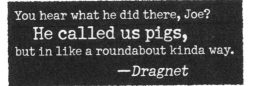

You hear what he did there, Joe?
He called us pigs,
but in like a roundabout kinda way.
—Dragnet

pig out, v.

to overeat; *American*

> Tracy always **pigs out** on chocolate and ice cream when she's PMSing.

piles, n.

hemorrhoids; *British*

> The worst thing about being up the duff is the **piles**.

> The worst thing about being knocked up is the **hemorrhoids**.

pillock, n.

fool; *British*

> Catherine, you **pillock**, don't forget to lock the door this time when you go out for your booty call.

> Catherine, you **fool**, don't forget to lock the door this time when you go out for your booty call.

pimp, n.

a man who manages prostitutes, taking a cut of their earnings; a guy who gets a lot of girls; *American*

> The **pimp** beat up two of his girls when they didn't give him half of the money they made.

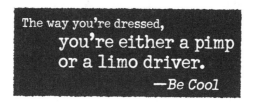

> The way you're dressed, you're either a pimp or a limo driver.
> —*Be Cool*

to pimp (out), v.

to make over something in an over-the-top way; *American*

> Check out that **pimped-out** low rider with the fuzzy dice hanging from the rear-view mirror.

> **DERIVATION:** Popularized by the MTV show *Pimp My Ride*.

pink truffle, n.

vagina; *American*

> Mary likes a man who knows his way around a **pink truffle**.

piss, v.

to urinate; *American*

> I didn't want to stop to take a leak, so I just **pissed** in a bottle while I was driving.

> **DERIVATION:** Piss comes from the Vulgar Latin *pissiare,* meaning to urinate. The French call a public urinal a *pissoir*; the perjorative *pissant* is a combination of *pismire* and *ant.* A *pismire* is an ant, named for the foul smell of its urine. We'll let Chaucer have the last word on piss:

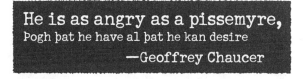

> He is as angry as a pissemyre,
> Pogh þat he have al þat he kan desire
> —Geoffrey Chaucer

piss off, v.

to anger; to get lost; *American*

> When you tell your wife she's fat, don't be surprised if you **piss** her **off** so much she tells you to **piss off**.

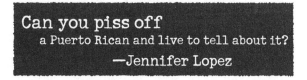

> Can you piss off
> a Puerto Rican and live to tell about it?
> —Jennifer Lopez

piss-ant, adj.

insignificant; *American*

> I might be a **piss-ant** loser, but your daughter wasn't complaining last night.

piss-poor, adj.

substandard; *American*

> This Kate Spade knock-off is a **piss-poor** substitute for the real handbag.

pissed off, adj.

upset; *American*

> I know you're **pissed off** that I forgot to pick you up from school today.

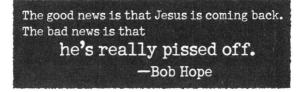

The good news is that Jesus is coming back. The bad news is that **he's really pissed off.**
—Bob Hope

pisser, n.

a jerk; bummer; toilet; *American*

> What a **pisser** that **pisser** passed out in your **pisser**.

pitch a tent, v.

to get an erection; *American*

> Trevor **pitched a tent** in class and everyone noticed— including his bootylicious teacher.

plank, n.

a fool; *British*

> With her track record, only a **plank** would be in a relationship with her.

> With her track record, only a **fool** would be in a relationship with her.

plastered, adj.

drunk; *American*

> Let's buy a couple of wine coolers and get **plastered**.

play with oneself, v.

to masturbate; *American*

> Shoshana was **playing with herself** when her boyfriend walked in and joined the game.

played out, adj.

unfashionable; no longer cool; *American*

> I can't believe you're going to wear a tight miniskirt . . . that look is so **played out**.

player, n.

a man who goes out or sleeps with many different women; *American*

> Todd slept with three girls this week? What a **player**!

You don't play a **player.**
—Firefly

plonker, n.

dummy; *British*

> If he weren't such a **plonker**, Stu would be able to fully appreciate the fit birds with the nice booties at the pub.

> If he weren't such a **dummy**, Stu would be able to fully appreciate the sexy girls with the nice booties at the bar.

pocket nymph, n.

a sexy, petite girl who one puts in his pocket, brings home, and turns into a sex slave; *American*

> At the bar there was this little **pocket nymph** I just wanted to throw in my shirt pocket and declare war on at my place.

poofy, adj.

effeminate; *British*

> Get rid of that **poofy** moustache. This is the army, not the Blue Oyster Cult.

> Get rid of that **effeminate** moustache. This is the army, not the Blue Oyster Cult.

poon/poontang, n.

pussy; *American*

> Last night I got so much **poontang** at the local brothel. That's why I'm in jail today.

pop a nut, v.

to ejaculate; *American*

> Despite his best intentions, Casey **popped his nut** inside his girlfriend a little too soon for her taste.

pop someone's cherry, v.

to break the hymen on a virgin's vagina; *American*

> Ricky **popped his girlfriend's cherry** and it stained the sheets. She made him change them.

posse, n.

a group of friends; clique; gang; *American*

> T-bone and his **posse** spent the night drinking forties and smoking ganja.

prairie dog, v.

to stand up in one's cubicle and peer out to view any excitement; *American*

> When the CEO yelled at me, all of the other workers **prairie dogged** me. It was so embarrassing.

prannet, n.

idiot, tool; *British*

> He's such a **prannet** that he probably needs a road map to find his wife's vagina.

> He's such an **idiot** that he probably needs a road map to find his wife's vagina.

prat, n.

jerk; *British*

> If you don't stop acting like a **prat**, I will never role play as a sexy French maid with a lisp again!

> If you don't stop acting like a **jerk**, I will never role play as a sexy French maid with a lisp again!

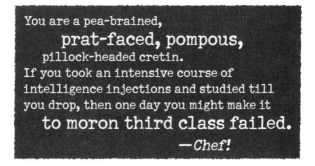

You are a pea-brained, **prat-faced, pompous,** pillock-headed cretin. If you took an intensive course of intelligence injections and studied till you drop, then one day you might make it **to moron third class failed.**
—*Chef!*

premature ejaculation, n.

when a man ejaculates before inserting his penis into his partner's vagina; *American*

> Brian bought a sybian for his wife to make up for his constant **premature ejaculations**.

premature evacuation, n.

being caught trying to sneak away after a one-night stand; *American*

> When he didn't realize how much he had drank and knocked into a wall, Todd woke up the chick he had slept with and suffered a **premature evacuation**.

prick, n.

penis; jerk; *American*

> Dating Rule #1: Once a **prick**, always a dick.

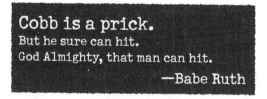

> Cobb is a prick.
> But he sure can hit.
> God Almighty, that man can hit.
> —Babe Ruth

prostitot, n.

an underage girl that dresses like a whore; *American*

> Mikey's little sister came in from school with a belly shirt and the shortest skirt ever, looking like a total **prostitot**.

pull, v.

to make out; to hit on; *British*

> You should try to **pull** Claire; she's well up for a bit of you.

> You should try to **make out** with Claire; she's totally into you.

punch up the bracket, v.

punch in the face; *British*

> Touch my wife again and you'll get a **punch up the bracket**, arsehole!

> Touch my wife again and you'll get a **punch in the face**, asshole!

pussy, n.

vagina; wimp; *American*

> Shut up, Dick, and lick my **pussy** now!

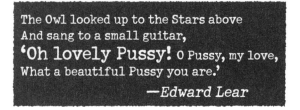

The Owl looked up to the Stars above
And sang to a small guitar,
'Oh lovely Pussy! O Pussy, my love,
What a beautiful Pussy you are.'

—*Edward Lear*

pussy-whipped, adj.

a man or lesbian who does everything their partner wants; *American*

> His wife makes him cook every night? Dude, Toby is **pussy-whipped**.

quack, n.

a bad, poorly trained doctor; *American*

> Oscar needs a hip replacement but won't let that **quack** near him.

queef, n.

vaginal fart; *American*

> I was about to go down on Megan until she let out this tiny **queef** in my face.

queer, n

homosexual; *American*

> No wonder Lee pushed Susanne away when she tried to French him—he's **queer**!

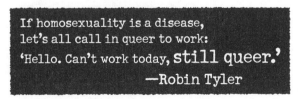

If homosexuality is a disease,
let's all call in queer to work:
'Hello. Can't work today, still queer.'
　　　　　　　　　　—Robin Tyler

quickie, n.

quick round of sex; *American*

> Jeremy caught his mom and dad having a **quickie** in the kitchen. He's had nightmares ever since.

With you, never a quickie. Always a longie.

—*Love at First Bite*

rack, n.

breasts; *American*

> That's some **rack** Marilyn Monroe had, I'll tell you.

➡ Top Ten Hollywood Racks

1. Marilyn Monroe
2. Scarlett Johansson
3. Mae West
4. Salma Hayek
5. Sophia Loren
6. Halle Berry
7. Jane Russell
8. Tyra Banks
9. Dolly Parton
10. Pamela Anderson

rag on (someone), v.

to criticize someone; *American*

> Stop **ragging on me**, Mom! I said I'd clean my room and I will!

rainbow kiss, n.

the act of going down on a woman when she is having her period; *American*

> I bet vampires have a fetish for giving **rainbow kisses**.

randy, adj.

horny; *British*

> I'm so **randy**, I'd fuck a horse . . . wait, that's not how the saying goes.

> I'm so **horny**, I'd fuck a horse . . . wait, that's not how the saying goes.

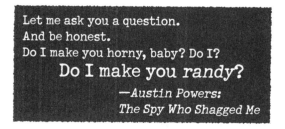

Let me ask you a question.
And be honest.
Do I make you horny, baby? Do I?
Do I make you *randy?*
—Austin Powers:
The Spy Who Shagged Me

razz, n.

puke; *British*

> Yuck! I've still got **razz** on my pants from that guy who didn't know his alcohol limits last night.

> Yuck! I've still got **puke** on my pants from that guy who didn't know his alcohol limits last night.

restroom, n.

break room; *British*

> Take a whiz in the **restroom** and you'll be sacked immediately.

> Take a whiz in the **break room** and you'll be fired immediately.

Richard, n.

poop, turd; *British*

> Move aside, I've got a **Richard** brewing that's likely to sound like an atomic bomb when it drops.

> Move aside, I've got a **turd** brewing that's likely to sound like an atomic bomb when it drops.

to ride, v.

to have sex; *American*

> Watch me **ride** the entire football team by the end of the season!

> ### Like you could ride me
> until my knees buckled.
> Squeeze me 'til I pop like warm champagne.
> That's not the kind of thing a man forgets.
> —*Buffy the Vampire Slayer*

ridin' dirty, n.

driving with illegal goods or drugs in one's car; *American*

> Don't let the pigs pull you over when you're **ridin' dirty** or you'll do jail time.

> ➡ If you're really into ridin' dirty, check out the classic Grammy-winning Chamillionaire song "Ridin'," which features rapper Krayzie Jones.

to rodger, v.

to have anal sex; *British*

> Oscar **rodgered** Bernadette and she couldn't walk the next day.

> Oscar **ass-fucked** Bernadette and she couldn't walk the next day.

root, v.

to have sex; *Australian*

> Avoid the toilets in the park after sundown. There are always a few blokes **rooting** in there.

> Avoid the toilets in the park after sundown. There are always a few dudes **having sex** in there.

ropey, adj.

ill or sick, often due to liquor; *British*

> After all that Guinness Alex drank, I'm not surprised he feels **ropey**.

> After all that Guinness Alex drank, I'm not surprised he feels **sick**.

rough, adj.

ugly; *British*

> That bird's as **rough** as nails, but she's rich so I see no reason why she couldn't at least be a sugar momma.

> That girl is **ugly** as shit, but she's rich so I see no reason why she couldn't at least be a sugar momma.

rub one out, v.

to jerk off; *American*

> He was watching a porno and **rubbing one out** when the power went out.

rumpy-pumpy, n.

sex; *British*

> I would enjoy a nice spot of **rumpy-pumpy** with her.

> I would like to have **sex** with her.

RX: SEX

A 42-year-old Dublin doctor was accused of malpractice after advising one of his insomniac patients to indulge in a little rumpy-pumpy to help her sleep. "Find a willy and have some sex," Dr. Ross Shane Ardill apparently told the woman, who later filed a complaint. The good doctor was cleared of all charges.

> 'Kinky rumpy-pumpy' is
> what my sergeant would call it.
> —Inspector Morse

rusty trombone, n.

the act of licking a man's anus while simultaneously reaching around and jerking him off; *American*

> Violet played the cello beautifully but refused to play the **rusty trombone**.

S

S&M

sadism and masochism; *American*

Jack and Jill may look like the All-American couple, but behind the closed doors of their classic Cape Cod home, they're totally into **S&M**.

SADE & MASOCH

S&M takes its name from two princes of penis envy, the Marquis de Sade and Leopold von Sacher-Masoch. The Marquis de Sade was a sexually obsessed eighteenth-century writer who glorified the pleasure of inflicting pain on one's sexual partner in his life as well as in such works as *Justine*, *Juliette*, and *The 120 Days of Sodom*. Arrested more than once for his writing and his actions, Sade spent much of his life in the asylum and prison. The term Sadism comes from the French *sadisme*, inspired by the Marquis de Sade. The renowned Austrian "Father of Psychoanalysis" Sigmund Freud popularized the term in 1905 in his *Three Essays on the Theory of Sexuality*.

Von Sacher-Masoch, on the other hand, was a nineteenth-century Austrian journalist, who played out his fantasies of sexual submission at home and on the page. His most famous "novel," *Venus in Furs*, tells the story of a man who persuades his wife to treat him as her slave with increasing degradation. (And yes, that eponymous song by The Velvet Undergound was inspired by this book.) The noted Austrian psychiatrist Richard Freiherr von Krafft-Ebing coined the term masochism after von Sacher-Masoch in his acclaimed treatise *Psychopathia Sexualis* in 1886.

scat, n.

sexual activity involving feces; *American*

> Thanks for your offer to shit on my face but I'll have to pass—I'm not really into **scat**.

schlong, n.

penis; *American*

> Jake has a foot-long **schlong**; I can hardly get it all into my mouth.

schmuck, n.

jerk; *Yiddish*

> Only a real **schmuck** would schtup your sister at your bar mitzvah.

> **DERIVATION:** The word *schmuck* comes from the Yiddish meaning penis.

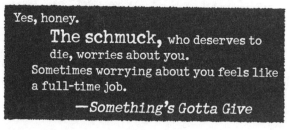

Yes, honey.
The schmuck, who deserves to die, worries about you.
Sometimes worrying about you feels like a full-time job.
—*Something's Gotta Give*

schtup, v.

to have sex; *American*

> Check out Lili von **Schtup** in that classic Mel Brooks
> western, *Blazing Saddles*.

> **DERIVATION:** The word *schtup* comes from the Yiddish
> meaning to press.

schwing, interj.

an expression meaning, roughly, "wow!" (usually
used in a sexual context); *American*

> When the nubile young Nicole walks into a room,
> every guy thinks, "**Schwing!**"—but only Davie is lame
> enough to say it out loud.

> **DERIVATION:** Popularized in the *Wayne's World* films
> featuring *SNL* alums Mike Myers and Dana Carvey.

screw, v.

to have sex; *American*

> Paul's **screwing** his blonde secretary? How bourgeois!

> My reaction to porno films is as follows:
> After the first ten minutes, I want to
> **go home and screw.**
> After the first twenty minutes,
> I never want to screw again
> **as long as I live.**
> —Erica Jong

screw up, v.

to mess up; *American*

> When Lonnie **screws up**, he screws up in a big way.
> That's why he's currently incarcerated.

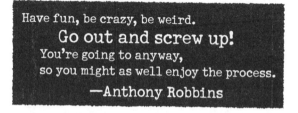

Have fun, be crazy, be weird.
Go out and screw up!
You're going to anyway,
so you might as well enjoy the process.
—Anthony Robbins

scumbag, n.

jerk; condom; *American*

> That **scumbag** Bobby always leaves his used
> **scumbags** lying around our dorm room.

If the First Amendment will
protect a scumbag like me,
it will protect all of you.
—Larry Flynt

see a man about a dog, v.

to go take a piss; *British*

> If you'll excuse me, ladies, I've got to **see a man about a dog**.

> If you'll excuse me ladies, I've got **to use the restroom**.

senioritis, n.

the lack of desire to attend school suffered by
high school seniors the spring before graduation;
American

> The principal just declared war on **senioritis**—any
> senior caught off school grounds during class hours
> will be suspended.

sex, n.

intercourse; gender; *American*

> **Sex** is a favorite extracurricular activity for all sexes.

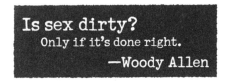

Is sex dirty?
Only if it's done right.
—Woody Allen

sex up, v.

to glamorize; *American*

> Sharlene always **sexes up** her life as a single woman
> whenever she talks to her married sister in Queens.

sexting, v.

sending nude photos via text; *American*

> Lorraine accidentally **sexted** four photos of her glorious double-Ds to her boss—instead of her boyfriend. She got a promotion.

shag, v.

to have sex; *British*

> There's nothing like **shagging** on a Sunday morning to start the Sabbath off right.

> There's nothing like **fucking** on a Sunday morning to start the Sabbath off right.

TO SHAG AN ENGLISHMAN

While the French may be known for their romantic ways and the Italians for their hot blood, the British may be the world's most underrated mates. Though they aren't known as particularly warm hearted or passionate lovers, recent surveys show they can indeed be counted on for a good *shag*. According to a *Men's Health* survey of over 40,000 men worldwide, British men spend more time on foreplay than any others, including the French and Italians. And, around one third of them say they bring their partner to orgasm every time they do the deed. On the other hand, the British devote only eighteen minutes to sex itself, embarrassingly less than the Mexicans and Dutch. Which explains why the terms "Mexican jumping bean" and "Dutch treat" are still in use . . .

shake the snake, v.

to drain the lizard; to pee; *British*

> This lager's going straight through me. I've got to go **shake the snake** again.

> This beer's going straight through me. I've got to go **drain the lizard** again.

shambles, n.

a mess; *British*

> Pete's marriage wouldn't be in **shambles** if he got over his fetish for S&M brothels.

> Pete's marriage wouldn't be a **mess** if he got over his fetish for S&M brothels.

shank, v., n.

to stab; a makeshift knife; *American*

> My friend spent a year in prison and almost got **shanked** by this guy who carved a knife from his toothbrush.

shed load, n.

shit load; *British*

> There's a **shed load** of pinched bangers in East London.

> There's a **shit load** of stolen cars in East London.

she-hulk, n.

a giant, frighteningly veiny penis; *American*

> I saw Fred in the locker room the other day out of the corner of my eye and his **she-hulk** hung past his knee; he could have killed me with it.

shigga digga, interj.

to show enthusiastic agreement or appreciation; *American*

> Paul told me this awesome story and said, "Know what I mean, dude?" All I could muster was, "Fuckin' **shigga digga**, man."

shit, n.

feces; stuff; jerk; *American*

> I hated my college roommate Sam—he never cleaned up and left his **shit** all over the apartment.

> **DERIVATION:** The word shit comes from the Old English *scite,* meaning dung.

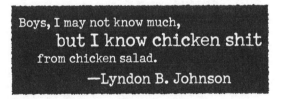

Boys, I may not know much, **but I know chicken shit** from chicken salad.
—Lyndon B. Johnson

shit, dawg!, interj.

an expression meaning, "wow!"; *American*

> **Shit, dawg**! You are so fucked now that you got your ass fired.

151

shit happens, interj.

an expression that means, roughly, "that's life"; *American*

> The hipster existentialist says with all the wisdom of his sixteen years on earth, "**Shit happens**, man, because life sucks."

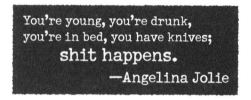

You're young, you're drunk,
you're in bed, you have knives;
shit happens.
—Angelina Jolie

shit list, n.

persona non grata; *American*

> Her lying, cheating ex-husband will be on Caroline's **shit list** for life.

shit on a stick, adj.

cool, great, fantastic; *British*

> You know what was **shit on a stick**? Bands usually stick the female of the group on any instrument but the guitar, but that fit bird was playing the guitar and rocking out.

> You know what was **great**? Bands usually stick the female of the group on any instrument but the guitar, but that biddy was playing the guitar and rocking out.

shit on someone, v.

to betray someone; *British*

> Divorce is just one spouse **shitting on the other person** for the last time—only in court.

> Divorce is just one spouse **betraying the other person** for the last time—only in court.

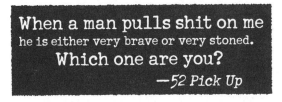

> **When a man pulls shit on me** he is either very brave or very stoned. **Which one are you?**
> —*52 Pick Up*

shite, n.

shit; *British*

> I was drinking straight shots of Jameson last night. Today, I feel like **shite** and have had explosive whiskey diarrhea all day.

> I was drinking straight shots of Jack Daniel's last night. Today, I feel like **shit** and have been taking whiskey shits all day.

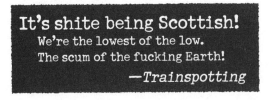

> **It's shite being Scottish!** We're the lowest of the low. The scum of the fucking Earth!
> —*Trainspotting*

shit-faced, adj.

drunk; *American*

> Pete came home totally **shit-faced** after a night of
> drinking with his old high school buddies.

shmonster, n.

general term for someone who isn't as good as you;
combination of "shmuck" and "monster"; *American*

> The biddy with the swoops is way too good for that
> **shmonster**.

shoop, v.

to fuck; *American*

> **Shoop** to Barry White—and you'll **shoop** some more.

shoot the shit, v.

to make small talk; *American*

> Tom **shoots the shit** so much on the job that he
> ends up doing a lot of overtime to catch up—on his
> employer's dime.

shop someone, v.

to snitch on someone; *British*

> That little rat **shopped me** for robbery. I'm going to
> rip his tongue out!

> That little rat **snitched on me** for robbery. I'm going
> to rip his tongue out!

shout, n.

round of drinks; *British*

> Mitch ordered another **shout** for the fit birds he was trying to seduce. However, he was ordering them O'Doul's and he soon left the bar that night, sans ladies.

> Mitch ordered another **round of drinks** for the biddies he was trying to seduce. However, he was ordering them O'Doul's and he left the bar that night, sans ladies.

shove off, v.

to go away; to get lost; *British*

> Tell that bloke who likes the New York Yankees to **shove off**—he probably overcompensates for his lack of a big bat by paying for his women with his over-exaggerated salary.

> Tell that dude who likes the New York Yankees to **get lost**—he probably overcompensates for his lack of a big bat by paying for his women with his over-exaggerated salary.

shysexual, n.

someone who shows little or no interest in sex of any kind; *American*

> Poor Theodore isn't just shy, he's **shysexual**.

sick, adj.

slang for cool; *American*

> If you think that's a **sick** monkey, look at this giant alligator—now that's ill.

sick, n.

puke; *British*

> When Patricia missed the toilet, she left **sick** all over the bathroom floor.

> When Patricia missed the toilet, she left **puke** all over the bathroom floor.

sick as a parrot, adj.

very disappointed; crushed; *British*

> Maria was **sick as a parrot** when her boyfriend told her he had rented *Beaches* but instead rented Takashi Miike's *Visitor Q*.

> Maria was **very disappointed** when her boyfriend told her he had rented *Beaches* but instead rented Takashi Miike's *Visitor Q*.

sideways smile, n.

an ass crack; *American*

> She bent over in these really low cut jeans and revealed her **sideways smile** to the whole place.

siphon the python, v.

to pee; *British*

> I'm going to **siphon the python** in the alleyway because it's closer than the bathroom in the restaurant.

> I'm going to **pee** in the alleyway because it's closer than the bathroom in the restaurant.

size queen, n.

one who places extreme importance on her or his partner's penis size; *American*

> Don't tell a **size queen** that you've got a big dick unless you're ready to pull down your drawers and prove it.

skank, n.

slut; reggae dance; *American*

> When that **skank** hit on my husband, I spilled my cosmo all over her Jimmy Choos.

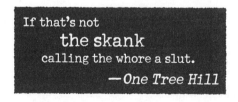

If that's not
the skank
calling the whore a slut.
—*One Tree Hill*

skanky, adj.

dirty; slutty; *American*

> **Skanky** is as **skanky** does.

> What, am I not
> ## skanky enough for you,
> you want me to hike up my fucking skirt?
> —*Knocked Up*

skeet, v.

to ejaculate; *American*

> It can be very hard to **skeet** when you're drunk off your ass.

skeevy, adj.

creepy; *American*

> When that **skeevy** guy kept hitting on Pamela, she had her boyfriend the bouncer toss him out of the bar and onto the street.

skid mark, n.

shit stain on underwear; *American*

> Underwear Rule #1: If you're leaving **skid marks**, wash your own underwear.

skin up, v.

to roll a joint; *British*

> I'm way too high to **skin up**, so you do it, you lazy prick.

> I'm way to high to **roll this joint**, so you do it, you lazy prick.

skins, n.

rolling papers; *British*

> Pass me the **skins** and I'll make us a joint, so we can properly watch *Pineapple Express*.

> Pass me the **rolling papers** and I'll make us a joint, so we can properly watch *Pineapple Express*.

skive off, v.

to cut class; *British*

> Screw geometry class—let's **skive off** and smoke some joints in the car park.

> Screw geometry class—let's **cut class** and smoke some joints in the parking lot.

slag, n.

slut; *British*

> Ian's such a loser even the **slags** won't chat him up.

> Ian's such a loser even the **sluts** won't talk to him.

slag someone off, v.

to bad mouth someone; *British*

> That bitch keeps **slagging me off**, so I started a rumor that she was a hermaphrodite and she still had both a penis and a vagina.

> That bitch keeps **bad mouthing me**, so I started a rumor that she was a hermaphrodite and she still had both a gun and a holster.

slapper, n.

slut, ho; *British*

> Mate, I'm only your friend because your sister is a **slapper** and I want to shag her.

> Dude, I'm only your friend because your sister is a **slut** and I want to fuck her.

Sloane Ranger

snob; *British*

> That art exhibit was full of **Sloane Rangers** drinking champers, but the joke was on them because there wasn't even any cheese and crackers there.

> That art exhibit was full of **snobs** drinking champagne, but the joke was on them because there wasn't even any cheese and crackers there.

➡ Sloane Rangers get their name from London's Sloane Square, located in the decidedly posh part of town most of them live in. Also refers to those well-paid individuals who work in the area. Rhymes with Lone Ranger . . . get it?

slob on someone's knob, v.

to give oral sex to a man; *British*

> In his dreams, Jack's girlfriend is always **slobbing on his knob**.

> In his dreams, Jack's girlfriend is always **blowing him**.

sloppy seconds, n.

the act of having sex with someone after that person has just had sex; *American*

> If you're going to have **sloppy seconds** with someone, you should ask that person to shower first. Or not, if you have a sweat fetish.

slore, n.

neologism combining slut and whore; *American*

> Where does a **slore** draw the line between prick-tease and prick?

slurry bucket, n.

any orifice in which a hand may be inserted; *American*

> She wanted me to fit my whole hand into the **slurry bucket** between her legs.

slut, n.

a promiscuous woman; *American*

> Ooh la la! Marie sees every business trip to Paris as a chance to be a **slut** with style.

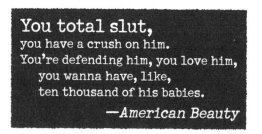

> **You total slut,**
> you have a crush on him.
> You're defending him, you love him,
> you wanna have, like,
> ten thousand of his babies.
> —*American Beauty*

smiling like a donut, adv.

opening one's mouth wide to perform oral sex on a man; *American*

> She **smiled like a donut**, but she really didn't have to because Harry had a really little dick.

smiling like a fish, adv.

opening one's mouth to perform oral sex; *American*

> After a long night of **smiling like a fish**, our jaws were sore—but our privates were happy.

snatch, n.

vagina; *American*

> That loser Larry is on the prowl for **snatch** every night—and every night he comes home empty-snatched.

snowball, v.

when after a blowjob, someone spits the cum into either the ejaculator's or someone else's mouth; *American*

> I came in my girlfriend's mouth, and as a prank, she kissed my roommate and **snowballed** him. He subsequently never looked at either one of us the same way again.

> After he gets a blowjob he likes to have it spit back into his mouth while kissing—
> ### it's called snowballing.
> —*Clerks*

soft lad, n.

softie (negative); queer; *British*

> If you're a greenhorn and a **soft lad** on *Deadliest Catch*, you are more than likely going to be rightfully berated and eventually fired.

> If you're a greenhorn and a **softie** on *Deadliest Catch*, you are more than likely going to be rightfully berated and eventually fired.

spank the monkey, v.

to masturbate; *American*

> Clarence couldn't answer the phone because he was **spanking the monkey**.

spare, adj.

at wits end; crazy; *British*

> Charlie's parents went **spare** when they found out he was dropping acid, but then mellowed out by smoking from their cannabis supply.

> Charlie's parents went **crazy** when they found out he was dropping acid, but then mellowed out by smoking from their cannabis supply.

spend a penny, v.

to go the bathroom; *British*

> Do you need to **spend a penny** before we set off because last time you pissed yourself?

> Do you need **to go to the bathroom** before we leave because last time you pissed yourself?

splash out on something, v.

to spend a lot of money on something; *British*

> We **splashed out on** Manolo Blahnik pumps and then the recession hit. Unfortunately, you can't eat shoes.

> We **spent a lot of money** on Manolo Blahnik pumps and then the recession hit. Unfortunately, you can't eat shoes.

spliff, n.

marijuana cigarette; *American*

> I just scored some kickass weed bro'—let's grab some beers and roll a **spliff** down at the lake.

Well, you don't roll like,
big rasta spliff joints,
do you? Your joints are like salad joints, not like a big, sloppy, bleeding cheeseburger-that-you-rip-into-kind-of-a-joint joint.

—*Igby Goes Down*

splooge, n.

semen; *American*

> Dirk shot his **splooge** on my tramp stamp last night.

spotty, adj.

pimply; *British*

> Today's **spotty** teenager is tomorrow's Cameron Diaz.

> Today's **pimply** teenager is tomorrow's Cameron Diaz.

squiffy, adj.

slightly drunk; *British*

> When Deloris gets **squiffy**, she gets very horny—so her husband keeps champagne on ice.

> When Deloris gets **slightly drunk**, she gets very horny—so her husband keeps champagne on ice.

squits, n.

diarrhea; *British*

> The **squits** that I just unleashed probably demolished the toilet in that restaurant.

> The **diarrhea** that I just unleashed probably demolished the toilet in that restaurant.

stag do, n.

bachelor party; *British*

> At Mitch's **stag do**, the boys shaved his bollocks and wrote "We Were Here" on them.

> At Mitch's **bachelor party**, the boys shaved his balls and wrote "We Were Here" on them.

stanky, adj.

stinky, smelly; *American*

> After ten days stuck at home with the stomach flu, Rob's apartment was beyond **stanky**.

starfish, n.

anus, asshole; *American*

> As I was banging her from behind and looking down at her **starfish**, all I could wonder was if she was into anal.

STD, n.

a sexually transmitted disease; *American*

> I went to this club that was so sketchy that I wouldn't
> have been surprised if I contracted an **STD** just by
> being in the proximity of the all those douchebags and
> sluts.

Stevie girl, n.

a loud, annoying drunk girl; an attention whore;
American

> The other night Cassandra turned into the ultimate
> **Stevie girl** and wouldn't shut up about her "crazy
> drinking stories."

sticky wicket, n.

sticky situation; *British*

> The moment he mentioned his other girlfriend,
> Charles knew he was in a **sticky wicket**.

> The moment he mentioned his other girlfriend,
> Charles knew he was in a **sticky situation**.

stitch up, v.

to con; *British*

> Chester **stitched** me **up** and left me with the bill
> for the brothel.

> Chester **conned** me and left me with the bill for
> the brothel.

stonker, n.

huge thing; *British*

> My lord! Your knob is a **stonker**, and might have its own zip code.

> My lord! Your knob is a **ginormous**, and might have its own zip code.

straight, adj.

heterosexual; *American*

> Are there any **straight** single guys left in San Francisco?

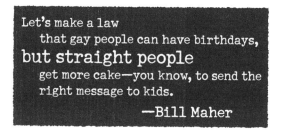

Let's make a law
    that gay people can have birthdays,
but straight people
    get more cake—you know, to send the
    right message to kids.
                    —Bill Maher

stroppy, adj.

irritating, annoying; *British*

> Georgina received a **stroppy** text from her boyfriend about his Asian fetish last night. Georgina is not Asian.

> Georgina received an **annoying** text from her boyfriend about his Asian fetish last night. Georgina is not Asian.

stubby, n.

small glass or bottle of beer; *Australian*

> I'll jam that **stubby** up your ass if you order another, one out of manly principle.

> I'll jam that **small glass of beer** up your ass if you order another, one out of manly principle.

stud muffin, n.

an attractive, fashionable guy who gets a lot of female attention; similar to pimp-daddy; *American*

> With his hot bod and square jaw, Brad Pitt is a total **stud muffin**.

stuff, v.

to have sex; *British*

> If you're lucky, you can get **stuffed** in London without eating a bite.

> If you're lucky, you can **have sex** in London without eating a bite.

succubus, n.

a demon who takes the form of a woman to have sex with men while they sleep; a needy, insecure girlfriend or wife who sucks away her significant other's soul and life; *American*

> After Lonnie married Margaret, we basically never saw him again because his **succubus** of a wife would scream at him if he even looked at another woman, much less was friends with ladies.

suck, v.

to be crappy; *American*

> My ex **sucked** at baseball. He was always more of a hockey man.

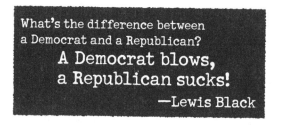

> What's the difference between a Democrat and a Republican?
> **A Democrat blows, a Republican sucks!**
> —Lewis Black

suck a fuck, v.

to tell someone to "fuck off"; sucking the after results of sex; *American*

> If you're not going to let me borrow your car so I can take your sister out for a nice time then destroy her, you can go **suck a fuck**.

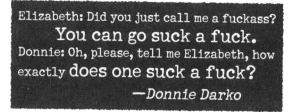

> Elizabeth: Did you just call me a fuckass? **You can go suck a fuck.** Donnie: Oh, please, tell me Elizabeth, how exactly **does one suck a fuck?**
> —*Donnie Darko*

suck someone off, v.

to perform fellatio on someone; *American*

> When Christine met Angelo at the wedding reception, by the third martini she was under the table **sucking him off**. Thank God for those long tablecloths.

suck up, v.

to appease; *American*

> Because he sucks at his job, Jack tries to make up for it by **sucking up** to his boss.

suckalicious, adj.

extremely attractive, meriting sucking; *American*

> Pamela's titties are **suckalicious**!

sugar daddy, n.

a well-off older man who dates younger partners; *American*

> There's no fool like an old **sugar daddy**.

sugar lumps, n.

small breasts; *American*

> Tony had a thing for girls with **sugar lumps**, so he loved Martha and her triple As.

sugar momma, n.

a well-off older woman who dates younger partners; *American*

> That **sugar momma** paid for my meal, then made me her meal in bed.

sundries, n.

freebies; *Australian*

> Our local take-away always gives us loads of **sundries** like free starters and drinks because our friend fucked the owner and she doesn't want anybody to know about it.

> Our local take-out always gives us lots of **freebies** like free appetizers and drinks because our friend fucked the owner and she doesn't want anybody to know about it.

swan sauce, n.

sweat that accumulates around a woman's vagina in the heat; *American*

> At the gym, Jerry goes for the girls who work out the hardest—he loves hard bodies swimming in **swan sauce**.

sweet, adj.

great, cool; *American*

> Your grandpa got you a **sweet** convertible for your sixteenth birthday? Sweet!

sweet as a nut, adj.

fine, just great; *British*

> How am I? Well, I just busted a nut, so I am **sweet as a nut**.

> How am I? Well, I just ejaculated, so I am **just great**.

switch hitter, n.

bisexual; *American*

> When Sam found out that his wife Kate was a **switch hitter**, he invited his lipstick-lesbian secretary over for dinner.

swoops, n.

bangs from one side of the forehead that go across the forehead and cover one eye; *American*

> Look at the girl with the **swoops** over there—she's like a hot cyclops!

tab, n.

cigarette; *British*

> She usually likes to smoke a **tab** before, during, and after we have sex—my kind of woman.

> She usually likes to smoke a **cigarette** before, during, and after we have sex—my kind of woman.

taco, n

pussy*; American*

> Pink tacos, fish tacos, whatever—there's no **taco** Marty won't eat.

take the mickey out of someone, v.

to mock someone; to pull someone's leg; *British*

> If John starts to **take the mickey out of you**, just tell him how awful his mother was in bed last night.

> If John starts to **mock you**, just tell him how awful his mother was in bed last night.

take the piss, v.

to make fun; *British*

> If you can't handle us **taking the piss** of you, you should learn to take it as well as you give it out.

> If you can't handle us **making fun** of you, you should learn to take it as well as you give it out.

talk shit, v.

talk nonsense; *American*

> The boss is always **talking shit** while we do all the real work.

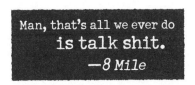

Man, that's all we ever do
is talk shit.
—8 Mile

talk to God on the big white telephone, v.

to vomit; *British*

> If you need to **talk to God on the big white telephone** when we get in my car, try to project your puke away from the side door.

> If you need to **puke** when we get in my car, try to project your puke away from the side door.

tart, n.

slut; *British*

> After we broke up, my ex still rang me twice a week for some nookie. What a **tart**!

> After we broke up, my ex still called me twice a week for some nookie. What a **slut**!

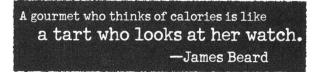

A gourmet who thinks of calories is like
a tart who looks at her watch.
—James Beard

tea bag, v.

to put one's testicles into someone's mouth or slap them on someone's face, sometimes unexpectedly; *American*

> We decided to **tea bag** Martin to get back at him for drinking all of our whiskey.

thick, adj.

dumb; *British*

> Martin the Mimbo is cute, but he's incredibly **thick**.

> Martin the Mimbo is cute, but he's incredibly **dumb**.

thicko, n.

dimwit; *British*

> Oi **thicko**, you usually wait for the band to start playing before you start a mosh pit.

> Hey **dimwit**, you usually wait for the band to start playing before you start a mosh pit.

thrombing, n.

a session of intense, aggressive sex; *American*

> We were both horny and pissed off, so I ripped her clothes off and gave her a hellacious **thrombing**.

throw a wobbly, v.

to throw a tantrum; *British*

> My boss **threw a wobbly** when he found out I'd quit. It was funny as fuck.

> My boss **threw a tantrum** when he found out I'd quit. It was funny as fuck.

tight ass, n.

a cheap or uptight person; also nice, firm buttocks; *American*

> Don't be such a **tight ass**—let me go down on you.

I'm gonna grab you by your Brooks Brothers PJs, and then I'm gonna take your brand new BMW, **and cram it up your tight ass!**
—*Caddy Shack II*

tits, n.

breasts; *American*

> There's nothing like a pair of babelicious **tits** to distract the boys.

> **DERIVATION:** Tit is one of the many variations of *teat,* which comes to us from the Old English *titt,* meaning breast. Take that into your mouth and suck it.

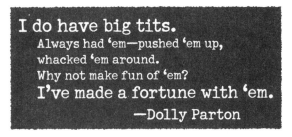

> **I do have big tits.**
> Always had 'em—pushed 'em up, whacked 'em around.
> Why not make fun of 'em?
> **I've made a fortune with 'em.**
> —Dolly Parton

tit for tat, interj.

an expression meaning, roughly, quid pro quo; *American*

> **Tit for tat** is the basis upon which all mutual pleasure should be founded—one orgasm at a time.

titty bar, n.

a strip club; *American*

> My friends and I went to the **titty bar**, but left because too many of the strippers had beef curtains.

titty fuck, v.

to rub one's penis between a woman's breasts;
American

> Nelly may be a goody-two-shoes virgin, but she still
> lets me **titty fuck** her.

todger, n.

penis; *British*

> Does that bloke have a third leg? Oh, wait, it's just his
> giant **todger**.

> Does that dude have a third leg? Oh, wait, it's just his
> giant **penis**.

toe cleavage, n.

the part of the toes exposed in low-cut shoes, usually
high heels; *American*

> There's nothing like a little **toe cleavage** to make a
> foot fetishist's day.

toe rag, n.

a loser; worthless person; *British*

> Stop being a little **toe rag** and jam those dollar bills in
> that stripper's G-string like you mean it.

> Stop being a little **loser** and jam those dollar bills in
> that stripper's G-string like you mean it.

tomtit, n.

shit; *British*

> I slipped in some **tomtit** but luckily I fell on my blow-up sex doll.

> I slipped in some **dog shit** but luckily fell on my blow-up sex doll.

tosser

jerk; *British*

> I will ram my car into that **tosser** who cut me off.

> I will ram my car into that **jerk** who cut me off.

tough titties, interj.

an expression meaning, "tough shit"; *American*

> Tara told Tom **tough titties** when he begged her forgiveness for feeling up her twin sister's tits on New Year's Eve.

> **DERIVATION:** We may have the pioneers to thank for this charming expression. The story is that on the long trek west on the wagon trail, tired moms gave their teething babies stale bread soaked in milk for their sore gums. They called them tough titties.

town bike, n.

town whore; *American*

> Lauren was well known as the **town bike** by everybody.

trade junk, v.

to have sex without commitment; *American*

> When you want to **trade junk**, just call a fuck buddy.

tradesman's entrance, n.

anus; rear door; *British*

> If a girl has just had Mexican food, you should avoid going in the **tradesman's entrance**.

> If a girl has just had Mexican food, you should avoid going up her **ass**.

trainspotter, n.

nerd, geek; *British*

> The **trainspotter** spent his time nitpicking the inaccuracies in *Star Wars* and dreaming of sex with Leia.

> The **geek** spent his spare time nitpicking the inaccuracies in *Star Wars* and dreaming of sex with Leia.

tramp, n.

a promiscuous woman; *American*

> Margaret may be fifty but she still dresses like a two-bit **tramp**.

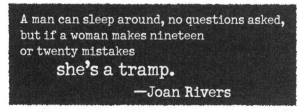

A man can sleep around, no questions asked, but if a woman makes nineteen or twenty mistakes **she's a tramp.**
—Joan Rivers

tramp stamp, n.

a tattoo placed on a woman's lower back; *American*

> One woman's **tramp stamp** is another woman's declaration of undying love—until she dumps the lying SOB and is stuck with his name forever.

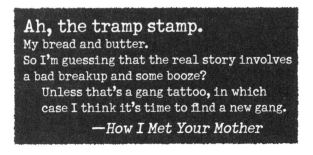

> **Ah, the tramp stamp.**
> My bread and butter.
> So I'm guessing that the real story involves a bad breakup and some booze?
>> Unless that's a gang tattoo, in which case I think it's time to find a new gang.
>
>> —*How I Met Your Mother*

tranny, n.

transsexual or transvestite; *American*

> When Barry took Barbie to bed, he was surprised to find out she was a **tranny**; Barry doesn't like surprises.

the trots, n.

the runs; *British*

> My girlfriend's mincemeat pie always gives me the **trots**, and after I've been in the bathroom for most of the night, she's never in the mood to have sex.

> My girlfriend's mincemeat pie always gives me the **runs**, and after I've been in the bathroom for most of the night, she's never in the mood to have sex.

trouser department, n.

penis; *British*

> My fiancé is a dear but he's seriously lacking in the **trouser department** and I have a dildo handy just in case he can't do the trick.

> My fiancé is a dear but he's seriously lacking a **large penis** and I have a dildo handy just in case he can't do the trick.

trustafarian, n.

a neologism combining trust fund and Rastafarian; young adult with a trust fund that allows him or her the financial security to work at a low-paying service industry job or follow his or her dream of becoming an artist or musician, all the while living a hippie lifestyle; *American*

> Williamsburg? Five years ago the place was super cool; now it's filled with **trustafarians** and wannabes.

tufted mussel, n.

an unshaved pussy; *American*

> Shakti Sunshine was a bit of a hippy and didn't believe in shaving down there, so she had quite a **tufted mussel**.

twat, n.

vagina; stupid, ignorant person; *American*

> There comes a time in every man's life when he needs to learn to tongue the **twat**. Good.

two dots and a dash, n.

penis and testicles; reference to Morse code; gay; *British*

> See that pre-op over there? She may have big tits but she's still got **two dots and a dash**.

> See that pre-op over there? She may have big tits but she still has a **penis**.

WAS MORSE GAY? Morse code has been used for more than 160 years to transmit information rhythmically. While it was used heavily in World War II, nowadays it's restricted mostly to amateur short wave radio operators. Perhaps this word entered the gay community via one of the hundreds of thousands of young sailors who served in the Navy during this time.

twinkie, n.

a person of Asian descent who more closely resembles white stereotypes; *American*

> Ji Yeon may be Korean, but she talks like a valley girl—what a **twinkie**.

DERIVATION: This term comes from the famed American snack food, the Twinkie. Twinkies, which are often mocked for their long shelf life, are oblong yellow cakes filled with creamy white filling. Hence the twinkie reference for Caucasian-acting Asian-Americans: yellow on the outside, white in the middle.

udder nonsense, n.

the act of fondling, groping, and sucking on breasts; *American*

> While the fucking was terrific, John equally enjoyed the **udder nonsense** with Brenda's perky boobs.

ululate, v.

to make a guttural response to intense sexual pleasure; *American*

> Mary polished Ted's knob so exquisitely that in turn he yodeled, **ululated**, and invoked the name of several saints.

umlauts, n.

breasts (from the German phonetic symbol of two dots over a vowel, usually U); *American*

> Appropriate given her Germanic lineage, Heidi had some nice **umlauts**.

unbutton the mutton, v.

to show one's penis; *American*

> James **unbuttoned the mutton** during their drive to the shore and asked Isla to give him road head.

Uncle Jim and the twins at attention, n.

the erect penis and testes; *American*

> By the time Tim got the flight attendant back to his apartment, there was swelling in his pants, which proved to be **Uncle Jim and the twins at attention**.

unclogging the drain, n.

female masturbation; *American*

> Paula let her husband know that she no longer needed his help in any respect: "Go out drinking with your buddies again, you son of a bitch, I'll be at home **unclogging the drain**, literally and metaphorically."

up the duff

pregnant, knocked up; *British*

> They've only been dating for a month, but Randy's girlfriend is already **up the duff**.

> They've only been dating for a month, but Randy's girlfriend is already **knocked up**.

V

vag, n.

short for vagina; *American*

> I may have a yeast infection. My **vag** is killing me.

vagina, n.

female sex organ; *American*

> The **vagina** is the passageway from which all emerge and many spend the rest of their lives trying to get back into.

> **DERIVATION:** The word vagina comes from the Latin meaning sheath.

SYNONYMS OF VAGINA:

baby gap	box	clunge
bacon strip	bucket hole	cock socket
bajingo	bush	cockholder
bearded clam	cake	coochie
beaver	cha cha	cooter
beef curtains	clam burger	crawl space
beetle bonnet	clown pocket	crumpet

cum dumpster

cunt

daisy

down there

downtown

downy bit

dugout

Elizabeth Regina

fanny

female parts

fish flaps

flapjacks

flower

foo foo

front bum

fur burger

furry goblet

gash

growler

guller buster

hair pie

hairy axe wound

hairy harmonica

ham wallet

holiest of holies

hoo-ha

joot

juicebox

kitty

lady bits

lady i-pod dock

lotus blossom

love canal

love pudding

mailbox

map of Tazzie

meow-meow

Mimi

minge

minky

mongo

monkey box

mud flaps

muff

mushmellow

nanner

noonie

Octo-mom exit

panties hamster

pee hole

pink taco

pleasure pit

poochie

poonanie

poontang

pound mound

powderbox

privates

pudding pot

pussy

quim

salmon canyon

skin chimney

slit

sloppy fun pocket

snatch

sperm sponge

split knish

sweetness

tamale

tooshed

tulip

tunnel of love

twat

twinkle

unit

whisker biscuit

wizard's sleeve

vag

vagine (à la Borat)

va-jay-jay

Virginia

VJ

you-know-what

> Honey, **my vagina** waits for no man.
> —*Sex in the City*

vaginal spaghetti, n.

a hairy vagina with dried menstrual blood; *American*

> She didn't change her pad and had a case of **vaginal spaghetti** when the blood dried up on her bush.

vagitarian, n.

one who enjoys cunnilingus; *American*

> Lou was a man's man, and a steak was often tempting, but when push came to shove he was a staunch **vagitarian**.

Vagoctopus, n.

a vagina, possibly of mythical origin, with tentacles; *American*

> Since my friend's wife is a succubus, I wouldn't be surprised if she had the mythical **Vagoctopus** that sucked his soul out with its tentacles of death.

va-jay-jay, n.

slang term for vagina; *American*

> Dora let her boyfriend know that her **va-jay-jay** was itchy, and if it was due to his infidelity with another, disease-ridden woman, she would cut off his dick, pan-fry it, and force feed it to him.

> **DERIVATION:** Popularized by Oprah, when she commented on her show: "I think **va-jay-jay** is a nice word, don't you?"

vanilla, adj.

conventional or boring sex; *American*

> I've got to dump Harold one of these days—the sex used to be hot, but now it's so **vanilla**.

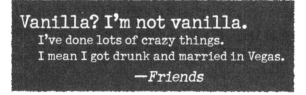

> **Vanilla? I'm not vanilla.**
> I've done lots of crazy things.
> I mean I got drunk and married in Vegas.
> —*Friends*

to veg out, v.

to relax, to zone-out; *American*

> We smoked a joint and spent the night **vegging out** and eating popcorn.

vertical smile, n.

slang term for vaginal lips; *American*

> He thought he'd stay awhile after seeing her **vertical smile**.

wacky backy, n.

pot, marijuana; *British*

> I can tell you've been smoking **wacky backy** because you've been dancing to Phish by yourself in the basement for the last hour.

> I can tell you've been smoking **pot** because you've been dancing to Phish by yourself in the basement for the last hour.

walk of shame, n.

when a person walks home wearing his or her clothes from yesterday (or someone else's clothes) and has a look on his or her face that he or she made a huge mistake by having sex with someone the previous night; *American*

> After sleeping with the girl who he had previously told his friends was a succubus, Mark did the **walk of shame** the next morning.

wang, n.

dick; *American*

> She wanted to see if that douche bag's **wang** was as large as he said it was; however, when she saw how small it was, she laughed at him and left.

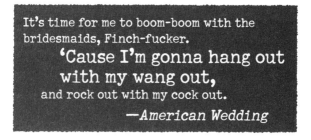

It's time for me to boom-boom with the bridesmaids, Finch-fucker.

'Cause I'm gonna hang out with my wang out,
and rock out with my cock out.

—American Wedding

wanker, n.

jerk-off; asshole; *British*

> If you want to continue being a **wanker**, you should keep talking gobshite to that dude who looks like he could break you in two.

> If you want to continue being an **asshole**, you should keep talking shit to that dude who looks like he could break you in two.

wannabe, n.

someone who tries desperately to impress others with their style, but fails; *American*

> Last Christmas morning I found my dad wasted in a Santa suit with an empty bottle of whiskey next to him. Some **wannabe** St. Nick he turned out to be.

war wound, n.

injury sustained during sexual congress; *American*

> Ted was a pantywaist draft dodger, but that didn't keep the sex maniac from sporting a bunch of **war wounds**.

Wassup?, interj.

slang term for "What's up?"; *American*

> Hey Dan, **wassup**? Been ages since we last talked.

➡ This expression was popularized by a Budweiser beer advertisement campaign that ran from 1999–2002.

wasted, adj.

inebriated; *American*

> When Don's dog died, he got **wasted** and watched *Old Yeller* over and over again.

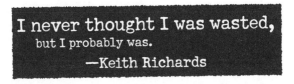

I never thought I was wasted, but I probably was.
—Keith Richards

waz, v.

pee; *British*

> The water closet was destroyed during last night's party, so just **waz** on the lawn.

> The bathroom was destroyed during last night's party, so just **pee** on the lawn.

wazzack, n.

idiot; *British*

> If you don't sleep with that bird with the sleeve tattoos, you are a complete and utter **wazzack**.

> If you don't sleep with that biddy with the sleeve tattoos, you are a complete and utter **idiot**.

wedding tackle, n.

junk; dick; *British*

> Frank spends half his life showing off his **wedding tackle**. It's not much to write home about.

> Frank spends half his life showing off his **penis**. It's not much to write home about.

wedgie, n.

when underwear gets pulled into the butt crack; *American*

> Only assholes give people **wedgies**. You should know.

weed, n.

marijuana; *American*

> Son, don't smoke too much **weed** or you'll grow up to be a loser like your father.

➥ **Top Five Weed Movies**
1. *Reefer Madness*
2. *Up in Smoke*
3. *Dazed and Confused*
4. *Half Baked*
5. *Pineapple Express*

wet, adj.

effeminate; *British*

> Richard is so **wet**; his girlfriend broke up with him two weeks ago and he's still crying.

> Richard is so **effeminate**; his girlfriend broke up with him two weeks ago and he's still crying.

wet dream, n.

dream during which a man ejaculates unconsciously; often occurs during puberty; *American*

> Johnny had a **wet dream** and tried to hide the stained sheets from his mom. Sadly, she found out anyway and told their preacher.

You're the only man I know who can **screw up his own wet dream.**
—*Flashpoint*

wet willy, n.

sticking a finger wet with spit in someone's ear; *American*

> All the school kids tortured the new girl by giving her **wet willies**.

whack off, v.

to masturbate; *American*

> Justin **whacks off** every night to an old '70s porno filled with hairy bushes.

whale eye, n.

anus; *American*

> The great, unwashed **whale eye** is just another dirty asshole.

whale tail, n.

the exposed top part of a girl's thong, which mimics the shape of a whale's tail; *American*

> There's this girl at my work who wears these low cut jeans with a thong every day, so I can see her **whale tail** whenever she walks past my desk.

whatchamacallit, n.

thing you don't know the name for; *American*

> Can you hand me that, oh, now I forgot the name, that **whatchamacallit** over there with the stripes?

whip it out, v.

to show one's penis; *American*

> Mary questioned the size of Joseph's wang, so he **whipped it out** so she could measure it.

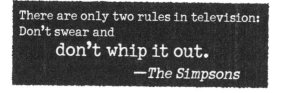

There are only two rules in television: Don't swear and **don't whip it out.**
—*The Simpsons*

whiskey dick, n.

the inevitable temporary erectile dysfunction
associated with too much alcohol consumption;
American

> We went back to my place, but I had a case of **whiskey
> dick**, so she left a bit unfulfilled.

whiskey shit, n.

the diarrhea that usually follows a night of drinking
whiskey; *American*

> After my ten Jack and Cokes last night, I woke up in
> the morning with a serious bout of **whiskey shit** that
> made me late for work.

white caps, n.

arrogant jerks who wear white hats, usually partially
slanted, at clubs; *American*

> We should brawl with those **white caps** and take
> their girlfriends.

to whizz one's tits off, v.

to get high as a kite (on speed, amphetamines);
British

> Jumping Alfie was **whizzing his tits off** and talking
> incoherently through his toothless mouth.

> Jumping Alfie was **getting high as a kite** and talking
> incoherently through his toothless mouth.

whore, n.

a prostitute; a woman who sleeps with many men; *American*

> Two fat **whores** in sweats work the street I live on.

> **DERIVATION:** The word whore comes from the Middle English *hore*, meaning adulterer.

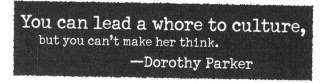

> You can lead a whore to culture, but you can't make her think.
>
> —Dorothy Parker

whore around, v.

to have sex with many people; *American*

> Thomas? The way he **whores around**, I wouldn't touch his dick with a ten-foot pole.

whinge, v.

to whine, complain; *British*

> Stop **whinging** and make me a sandwich now.

> Stop **whining** and make me a sandwich now.

willy, n.

penis; *American*

> Stuart never forgot the one time he zipped up too quickly, lacerating his **willy**. He wore button-fly slacks for the rest of the decade.

wingman, n.

a guy who assists his friend with getting a hot girl, by occupying her less attractive friend; also, a person who talks up his friend to a hot girl or starts a conversation with her then passes her on to his friend; *American*

> My friend was a perfect **wingman** because he started talking to this hot biddy then passed her on to me; unfortunately, she thought Bear Grylls was better than Les Stroud, so I decided I didn't want to have sex with her anymore.

winking, v.

when a girl with no panties accidentally flashes her vagina to a room full of people; *American*

> Virginia jumped on me at the bar and fell over; unfortunately, she was wearing a skirt and no panties and **winked** at the whole room.

womyn, n.

militant feminist; lesbian spelling of woman; *American*

> This chick at a bar was telling me about how men created the language so they've controlled it since the beginning of time, and I immediately asked, "Wait, do you spell woman, **w-o-m-y-n**?"

➥ This spelling uses a 'y' as a reference to the Y male chromosome.

woody, n.

erection; *American*

> Woody's **woody** bulged in his jeans—and the women swooned.

woofter, n.

homosexual; *British*

> I don't want to worry you, but I think your boyfriend may be a **woofter** because he always seems to want a dick in his mouth.

> I don't want to worry you, but I think your boyfriend may be a **homosexual** because he always seems to want a dick in his mouth.

WTF, interj.

acronym for "what the fuck"; expression used to describe a messed up situation; *American*

> When Maxwell wanted me to shove a dildo up his ass and call him "Sally," I was like "**WTF?**"

X, n.

the drug ecstasy; *American*

> I can't go to the rave without scoring some **X** first . . .
> otherwise I won't be able to dance all night.

XXX, n.

film rating given to the most sexually explicit movies,
by their makers; *American*

> This ain't no **XXX**! I have some dead wood here.

A BRIEF HISTORY OF PORN

in November of 1968, bowing to pressure, mostly from religious corners, the Motion Picture Association of American (MPAA) put in place a voluntary rating system to alert film goers of sexual themes, strong language, and violence. The now-familiar ratings of G, PG, R, and NC-17 (formerly X) were put in place. PG-13 was added later. Screenwriters and filmmakers avoided X marking their spot as that would sink all hope of a gold statue. But for the purveyors of golden showers on film, the porno industry, they not only embraced the X, but also beefed it up by putting it to the third power, XXX.

xanthodont, n.

a person with yellow teeth; *American*

> Anna said she really enjoyed fucking the carnival geek because, as she put it, he was hung like a garden hose about to burst, but had to break it off because he was a real **xanthodont**.

XDR, n.

cross-dresser; *American*

> When Harold admitted that he'd been seeing an **XDR** at night, his wife thought he meant a new Ferrari.

xenobiotic, n.

substance or item foreign to the body; *American*

> For the two lesbians happily in love, the twenty-three-inch black mambo dildo and their mate's fist were not off limits, but actual penises were strictly **xenobiotic**.

xenofuckic, adj.

afraid to be intimate with foreigners; *American*

> Suzy used to go down on a lot of foreign women, but after a bad Lithuanian experience she became **xenofuckic**, and now only eats Presbyterian pie.

xeric, adj.

dry, devoid of moisture and lubrication, as in the vaginal cavity; *American*

> Before there's any humpin' and bumpin', we gotta get some KY jelly for your **xeric** vagina.

Y

to yack, v.

to vomit; *American*

I had some bad fish and wound up **yacking** for about half an hour and wasn't in the mood to give any blowjobs to my boyfriend.

yada yada yada, n.

meaning "blah blah blah" or "etc., etc., etc."; used to quickly skip sections or avoid going into details while telling a story; *American*

I thought she seemed like a conservative girl, we had dinner, went back to my place. **Yada yada yada**, I woke up chained to my bed with my body shaved and a burlap sack over my head.

➡ This term was popularized during the long-running comedy series *Seinfeld*.

yellow fever, n.

an interest and attraction toward Asian women; *American*

> Hal's got **yellow fever** so bad, he has threatened to just move to Tokyo.

youniverse, n.

the belief by a narcissist that the universe revolves around him or her; *American*

> If James realized aliens didn't really abduct and anoint him "Supreme Emperor of the Universe," his **youniverse** would come crashing down to reality.

yuppie, n.

young, urban professional; often drives a BMW or Mercedes and shows off material wealth; *American*

> No offense, but most bankers are total BMW-driving **yuppie** assholes.

yupscale, adj.

used to describe a young professional who pretentiously shows off his or her wealth to gain attention; the word is a combination of "yuppie" and "upscale"; *American*

> Rick really showed his superiority complex with his **yupscale** apartment, so I banged his wife and ejaculated all over his expensive furniture.

yupster, n.

a combination of yuppie and hipster; a hipster who, while remaining faithful to some hipster elements such as music or neighborhood, has embraced a yuppie career or lifestyle; *American*

> When Matt gave up his gig as a DJ to concentrate more on his day job as an accountant, we knew that despite keeping his studio in Williamsburg he had crossed the **yupster** line.

YUPSTERVILLE

Williamsburg, Brooklyn is a neighborhood in New York City, which has a high population of hipsters, vegetarian cafes, bars, organic grocery stores, and vintage clothing shops. The area, once a mecca of crime in the early 1980s, has seen one of the fastest gentrifications in urban history and is now filled with so-called trustafarians, young adults with trust funds that allow them the financial security to work at low-paying service industry jobs or follow their dreams to be an artist or musician, while living a hipster lifestyle.

yutz, n.

an idiot; dolt; *American*

> Don't be a **yutz**, she obviously likes you, so go over there and fuck her brains out.

It's a nightmare, we've been visited by the
Yutz of Christmas Past.
—*The Golden Girls*

Z

zab, n.

penis; *American*

> After inspecting the lesions on the underclassman's manhood, the hip campus doctor assured him the blood work was negative, then pulled out a balm and told him to "just put a dab on your **zab** each morning."

zebra act, n.

an interracial couple; *American*

> These days dating and marriage by people of different races is generally accepted and not commented on, but my ancient Uncle Don still calls it a **zebra act**.

zeig heils, n.

hemorrhoids; *British*

> The jogger rarely had running cramps, but in long road races often found himself with a humdinger case of **zeig heils**.

> The jogger rarely had running cramps, but in long road races often found himself with a humdinger case of **hemorrhoids**.

zeps, n.

large breasts (short for zeppelins); *American*

> Steve always went to that particular ticket clerk's window as she featured a near-perfect pair of **zeps**.

zipper skipper, n.

a homosexual; *American*

> I thought he was just bored with my anecdote when he was staring down, but I'll be damned if that **zipper skipper** wasn't staring at my package!

zipper spark, v.

dry humping with your clothes on; *American*

> They were so hot for one another that they **zipper sparked** in the car in front of her parents house until her dad came out to get her.

to zone out, v.

to daydream; to be lost in one's own world; *American*

> Sorry, man, could you repeat that? I **zoned out** there for a minute.

zoosexual, n.

a person who prefers sexual activity with animals; *American*

> If you don't believe **zoosexuals** exist, you just have to watch some German porn or a Tiajuana donkey show.

Resources

Bernstein, Jonathan. *Knickers in a Twist: A Dictionary of British Slang.* Edinburgh: Canongate Books, Ltd., 2006.

Bryson, Bill. *The Mother Tongue.* New York: HarperCollins, 1990.

Vallardi, Editore Antonio. *Inglese Slang.* Milan: Antonio Vallardi Editore, 2003.

Miall, Anthony and David Milsted. *Xenophobe's Guide to the English.* London: Oval Books, 2008.

www.abc.com

www.aldertons.com/english.htm

www.brainyquotes.com

www.cbs.com

www.cockneyrhymingslang.co.uk

www.coolslang.com

www.imdb.com

www.madonna.com

www.manchestereveningnews.co.uk/news/health

www.phrases.org.uk

www.probertencyclopaedia.com

www.urbandictionary.com

www.thinkexist.com

www.usnews.com

www.wordreference.com